# Dr. Gott's No Flour, No Sugar™ Cookbook

# Dr. Gott's No Flour, No Sugar™ Cookbook

PETER H. GOTT, MD

**WELLNESS
CENTRAL**

NEW YORK   BOSTON

This book is not intended as a substitute for the medical advice of physicians. The reader should regularly consult a physician in all matters relating to his or her health, and particularly with respect to any symptoms that may require diagnosis or medical attention.

Wellness Central
Hachette Book Group USA
237 Park Avenue
New York, NY 10017

Visit our Web site at www.HachetteBookGroupUSA.com.

Wellness Central is an imprint of Grand Central Publishing. The Wellness Central name and logo is a trademark of Hachette Book Group USA, Inc.

Printed in the United States of America

First Edition: January 2008
10 9 8 7 6 5 4 3 2

Library of Congress Cataloging-in-Publication Data
Gott, Peter, 1935-
   Dr. Gott's no flour, no sugar cookbook / Peter H. Gott.—1st ed.
      p. cm.
   Includes index.
   ISBN-13: 978-0-446-58250-6
   ISBN-10: 0-446-58250-6
   1. Sugar-free diet—Recipes. 2. Reducing diets—Recipes. I. Title.
   RM237.85.G67 2007
   641.5'63837—dc22
                                                   2007015895

Book design by Charles Sutherland

# CONTENTS

# ACKNOWLEDGMENTS

I extend grateful thanks to Linda Kay Hardie, Pat Miller, and Stephen Blake Mettee for their loyalty and support in getting this book completed. I wish to thank Natalie Kaire and her staff for their interest, commitment, and editorial professionalism. Special thanks go to April Miller for her insight and dedication. Her contribution and skills made this project possible.

# INTRODUCTION

I recently completed my fortieth year of medical practice and have written a nationally syndicated Q & A medical column for a great portion of that time. I receive about twenty-five hundred letters with questions on a great variety of topics each week. The one question I am asked repeatedly by my readers is how to lose weight sensibly without indulging in impossible to maintain and, ultimately, futile diets.

Statistics reveal that 60 percent of American adults are overweight and I feel this problem should be actively addressed. Obesity is responsible for more than three hundred thousand deaths annually in the United States alone, and costs the country more than $170 billion annually in medical expenses, according to the National Center for Chronic Disease Prevention and Health Promotion. Numerous medical studies reveal that being overweight limits your energy levels and your feeling of well-being, and impairs your health. Moreover, several medical studies have confirmed that reduced consumption of simple carbohydrates will improve general health. (See chapter 2 for an explanation of simple versus complex carbohydrates.) I am aware that most people cannot fit into the same clothes that they wore in high school or college (nor would they want to wear them). Our frames haven't changed, so why have our weights?

Any number of reasons may explain the stretching of our waistbands. Restaurant food portions are supersized, and fast-food chains are available on every street corner. We are tempted to take the easy way out and tend to indulge in the wrong foods. In today's society, both parents in a family may work, leaving less time for meal planing and provision. No one wants to come home after a long day at work and begin time-consuming meal preparation. We may not have been organized enough over the weekend to fill the freezer with well-balanced casseroles that we can just microwave. Nor did we stop by the supermarket for simple fixings from which to toss together something nutritious. Some members of our family may still complain when presented with healthful meals. Others may say they don't get enough to eat. In the end it appears easier to pick up supersized fast food on the way home and attempt to please everyone. No fuss, no muss. But, this is a decision with long-term consequences!

## Silver Bullet?

We yearn for a magic pill that will make us shed our unwanted pounds. We try every diet available—including grapefruit, low-fat, no-fat, low-carb, no-carb, high-protein, and more.

One problem with these fad diets is that they are extremely restrictive and most aren't healthful. A very high-protein diet stresses the kidneys and liver, forcing these organs to work harder to process and excrete the excess nitrogen proteins contain. The risk of osteoporosis is elevated, because high-protein diets lead to calcium excretion. Further, these diets tend to be low in cholesterol-lowering fiber.

Diet plans that require specific foods be purchased are often expensive. The household food preparer may end up making an individual meal for him- or herself and feed the family a different array of foods. This is time consuming and many, especially parents on the go, simply haven't the inclination to follow through.

Fad diets promise fast, dramatic results, and they often deliver on that promise. Initially, a few pounds are shed. This is followed by cyclic eating binges, and the weight is back on. It's what I call the yo-yo plan. Up and down. Lose a little, gain a little. This simply doesn't work in the long run. Additionally, keep in mind that many fad diets can be detrimental to your overall health because, as you are dieting, you aren't getting the nutrients your body requires.

## It's Your Body

As I mentioned above, people who are overweight experience limits in energy levels and in feelings of well-being, and carrying around extra pounds impairs their health. Extremely overweight individuals have a greater than 70 percent chance of having an obesity-related health issue—coronary artery disease, hypertension, diabetes, high cholesterol levels, and certain types of cancer. These facts have been proven statistically by many medical studies. You can remove yourself from being such a statistic by taking simple measures to control your consumption of the wrong foods. Take the first step and reduce the amount of simple carbohydrates in your diet. What better reason than your health do you need to confront the issue now?

## The No Flour, No Sugar Diet

Several years ago, with the assistance of my overweight patients, I developed a diet to help people lose weight. This was followed in 2006 by the publication of my book *Dr. Gott's No Flour, No Sugar Diet*. People responded by the thousands that they had finally found a program they could stick to effortlessly. It remains simple, flexible, inexpensive, safe, and effective, and it enables people to regain control of their lives. Readers continue to report that aside from weight loss, their diabetes has been under better control without additional medicine, their cholesterol levels have dropped, and their blood pressure readings have been lowered. On my diet, the reduction is gradual, but consistent.

What could be easier? Simply put, you eliminate flour and sugar from your diet. There is no calorie or carb counting, and what makes my diet work is that, on occasion, cheating is allowed and even endorsed, providing you diet well in advance of your indulgence.

After publishing *Dr. Gott's No Flour, No Sugar Diet*, I received thousands of letters from readers asking for additional recipes that would allow them to follow the diet. My response is this cookbook.

## Reasons for Overeating

Some individuals are predisposed to being overweight and may have a more difficult time losing unwanted pounds. Family history plays an important role in obesity, ranging from genetic components to learned eating and exercise habits. While there are genetic and hereditary causes, there are also lifestyle and psychological causes. We need to understand better the role genetics and heredity play. We can control how much we eat, how often we eat, what we eat, and how consistently we exercise. Stress, depression, anger, and loneliness are common responses used to justify eating more than is necessary or practical. We've all seen television programs where an individual is shown eating a pint of ice cream as comfort food rather than addressing the issue at hand. Well, it's not too late to learn better approaches to more healthful eating habits, and I will work with you toward this goal.

My program is more than a diet. It is a sensible guide for healthful eating that will help you achieve your goal—and maintain it. It does not require counting calories or grams of carbs, memorizing lists of acceptable foods, or struggling with complicated food combinations. The key to weight loss is simple—burn more calories than you consume.

## Substituting High for Low

The No Flour, No Sugar Diet works because replacing high-calorie carbs with low-calorie vegetables and fruits reduces your daily intake of calories. Flour and sugar are both carbohydrates that add excessive calories and no nutritional value to what you eat.

One pound of fat is roughly equal to 3,500 calories. In order to lose one pound a week, you must reduce your calorie consumption by 500 calories each day. How can this be done? Adhere to my No Flour, No Sugar Diet.

This doesn't mean you will walk away from the dinner table hungry. Whole grains and starchy vegetables such as brown rice, barley, corn, and potatoes will add bulk to your meals. You can still enjoy meats, cheeses, and even an occasional glass of wine or your favorite cocktail.

Snack on raw vegetables. In fact, sliced and ready-to-eat carrots, celery, green or red peppers, and other favorites will provide a fast, healthful snack immediately available when you open your refrigerator door. Want dessert? Try an apple or other fresh fruit. In fact, try a medley of apples, melon, pineapple, grapes, or whatever the season offers in your section of the country. Cutting out "empty" calories— those with little or no nutritional value—is a simple and painless way to move toward your goal.

Do a little bit extra and take a walk or exercise for at least a half hour every day. If you choose not to leave your home in the evening after dinner, get on a treadmill during the evening news. You'll accomplish two things at once—you'll be keeping up on world affairs and keeping down your weight!

## Embrace Success

How do I know my formula works? I have received thousands of letters from my readers indicating they finally have a plan that is easy to follow. Success stories abound—and I've included some in this book.

The dishes you'll find here are nutritious and easy to follow and will create surprisingly positive results. You can treat your dinner guests to meals that are attractive, tasty, and good for them such as the Mediterranean Bean Wraps made with feta cheese, basil, and lime juice with Crème Brûlée for dessert. You'll be able to give your family the best gift ever—the chance at a longer and healthier life. If you live alone, give yourself that gift. You can do it. I can lead you in the right direction, but the rest is up to you.

# Part I

*The No Flour, No Sugar Diet*

# How to Thrive on the No Flour, No Sugar Diet

Thousands of people say that my No Flour, No Sugar Diet is the simplest and easiest diet they have ever tried. To start, there are only four words to remember: no flour, no sugar. This means no diet stages to get confused with, no food scales to use, and no calories to count.

Still, many people struggle with the finer points of the diet. I frequently get questions such as "Is honey okay for me to substitute for sugar in my tea?" "I really love cheese, but I know it is high in fat. Can I eat as much cheese on the No Flour, No Sugar Diet as I please and still lose weight?" "I know fruit has a lot of natural sugar in it. But I love it. Do I have to stay away from fruit?"

So let's answer these questions and then let's talk a bit about how you can welcome the No Flour, No Sugar Diet into your daily life.

## Is Honey Okay?

My diet is designed to help you avoid concentrated sugars that have been added to the foods you eat, as well as sugars you add yourself. They include molasses, cane sugar, maple sugar, corn syrup, and honey. Not only are these items high in fat-causing calories, but they also provide nearly no nutritional benefits. If you feel you need to sweeten your tea or coffee, I suggest you substitute Splenda, a calorie-free sweetening agent derived from sugar.

## So I Can Eat All I Want as Long as There's No Flour, No Sugar?

Can you eat all you want? Yes and no. Yes, by following my No Flour, No Sugar Diet you will find you are eating enough to satisfy your hunger cravings, but that doesn't mean you can throw caution to the wind. For instance, eating a pound of Brie cheese each day or dining on fat-laden sausages at every meal isn't smart. Yes, cheese and sausage are permitted on my diet, but use a little common sense. You still must watch the quantities of foods you eat that are high in fat content. A good idea is to substitute low-fat versions of these foods. Some great low-fat sausages, most made with turkey or soy, are now coming on the market and excellent low-fat cheeses have been available for years. As always, moderation is the key.

Many markets are now stocking flourless breads that also have no sugar, salt, or oil. As a bread substitute, whole-corn tortillas (made with corn, not corn flour) work well.

## Fresh Fruit?

Fresh fruit is encouraged on my diet. This is an ideal way to satisfy your sweet tooth. Be wary of canned fruit since many have sugar added or are packed in syrup. Fresh fruit is relatively low in calories and is nutrient dense. It is hard to imagine how anyone could eat too much fresh fruit.

## Use the Recipes in This Book

A useful step in adjusting to the diet is to use the recipes in this book. First try them exactly as they are here, then experiment on your own substituting one ingredient or spice for another. Just make sure any new ingredients have no flour and no added sugar. Note that some recipes in this book are attributed to others. These are recipes that I've received from people on the diet who happened to create an original, delicious recipe that fits within the parameters of the No Flour, No Sugar Diet.

## Make Your Kitchen No Flour, No Sugar–Friendly

Cornstarch is a good flour substitute for thickening foods and can be purchased in a one-pound package. Keep a box on hand for the times you might require it. Either get rid of that bag of flour in your pantry or transfer it to a canning jar or other container with a sealed top. Place this container in a little-used cupboard or on an upper shelf that lacks easy access. Out of sight, out of mind.

Sugar is found on many kitchen tables and is used on everything from cereals to desserts. Remove the temptation to use it in the same way as you dealt with the flour. Empty the sugar canister into a container with a sealed top. Place it next to the flour and close the door.

If you have guests coming over for a cup of coffee who insist on sugar, buy individual serving packets to put out just when they are there. Of course, since 60 percent of Americans are overweight, chances are your guests are too. Try serving a sugar substitute such as Splenda. You might as well get your guests on the right track too.

## Ditch the Cookies

Do you have a supply of cookies and pastries in the cupboard you simply hate to throw away? Or bags of candy? Eating these items to keep them from going to waste is definitely not the best approach. You could seal them in small bags and place them in your freezer to save for when you have guests over, but you might still be tempted knowing they were there. My advice is to go through your pantry and refrigerator checking ingredient labels. Pull out any foods made with flour or sugar. Throw away the open containers and box up the rest to donate to a charity.

Does this seem wasteful? Think of the money you'll be saving on medical bills by getting to and staying at a proper weight.

## Replace Comfort Foods with Intelligent Alternatives

A new you has taken charge. You can say no to those items you once considered comfort foods. Do you have ice cream in your freezer? Would you be surprised to learn that half a cup of some kinds of ice cream contains 280 calories? These calories come from the high fat content inherent in the dairy products the ice cream is made from and from sugar added by the manufacturer. A refreshing substitute is one of the excellent unsweetened, low-fat or fat-free frozen yogurts available at the supermarket, or you could make your own Popsicles by freezing fruit juice in small cups.

Check out the dessert recipes in chapter 17 for some other comfort food alternatives, and feel free to experiment with these on your own.

## Shop with a Grocery List

Now comes the fun—shopping. It's time to make a grocery list. Look over the recipes in this book and decide which ones you'll try first. Add their ingredients to the list. Don't forget extra fruits and vegetables, which make ideal snacks.

Always have a snack before grocery shopping. Shopping hungry often leads to spontaneous purchases of sugary or fatty foods. By having a snack beforehand, you can keep your mind on your list and not on a rumbling stomach.

Stick to the list when you get to the store. Buy lean meats and low-fat cheeses. You'll soon become a pro at this and it won't take long before you whip past the shelves offering fattening goodies without as much as a second thought.

Removing the temptation from your cupboards, refrigerator, and freezer is to take control of your life. Start today. You will be grateful you did.

# The Place of Carbohydrates in Your Diet

Because I believe we all need to understand more about our diets and our health in general so we can make informed decisions for ourselves and our families, I want to spend some time clearing the air regarding carbohydrates, especially because of the controversy and confusion we encounter regarding low-carb diet fads.

Carbohydrates come from a wide array of foods including bread, potatoes, cookies, pasta, and more. Our digestive systems break down carbs into single sugar molecules, as only these are small enough to pass into the bloodstream. Most digestible carbs are converted into blood sugar and used for energy. The exception to this is fiber, which is put together in such a way that it can't be broken down into sugar molecules. Fiber passes through our bodies undigested.

## Two Forms

Carbs have long been presented in two basic forms—simple and complex. Simple carbs contain up to three units of sugar linked together in single molecules and include regular table sugar and high-fructose corn syrup, found in many prepared foods. Traditionally these have been classified as "bad" sugars. They are a source of what people call "empty calories," meaning calories devoid of nutrients. Simple carbs are easy to identify by their sweet taste.

Complex carbs often contain thousands of sugar units linked together in single molecules. Complex carbs usually taste good but aren't sweet per se. Examples of complex carbs include potatoes, pasta, and other flour products. These have traditionally been considered "good" in comparison with the "bad" carbs. We now know this view is too simplistic.

## Glycemic Index

One way to classify carbs is known as the glycemic index or GI, which measures how fast blood sugars rise after a person eats carbohydrates. For example, white bread is immediately converted to blood sugar, causing a rapid spike. It is thus classified as having a high GI. According to recent studies, consumption of foods with high GI levels has been linked to an increased risk of heart disease and diabetes, while lower GI foods have been proven to help control type 2 diabetes. Glycemic indexes of 70 and above are considered high, while 55 or less are low.

An important factor in the determination of the GI of a food is how highly processed its carbs are. Processing removes the fiber-rich outer layers and the vitamin and mineral rich inner germ, leaving starch. Thus, finely ground grain has a higher GI and is more rapidly digested than is more coarsely ground grain.

Another determining factor of how quickly carbs raise blood sugars is how ripe fruits and vegetables are when eaten. Ripe ones have more sugar than those that are unripe, and therefore have a higher glycemic index.

One thing a food's glycemic index does not tell us is the relative amount of carbohydrates in any given food. Therefore, looking at the GI alone may not tell us all we need to know. Researchers now take into account the amount of carbohydrates in a food, as well as the impact they may have on blood sugar levels. This is expressed in terms of a glycemic load or GL. A food's glycemic load is determined by multiplying the GI by the grams of carbohydrates in an average serving of that food. A low GL is considered to be 10, while a GL of 20 or above is considered high.

Table 2.1 shows examples.

**TABLE 2.1**

| Food | Glycemic Index | Glycemic Load |
|------|----------------|---------------|
| ½ cup cooked instant rice | 91 | 16 |
| ½ small (3") bagel | 72 | 11 |
| 1 slice white bread | 70 | 9 |
| 1 slice whole wheat bread | 69 | 9 |
| ½ cup carrots | 92 | 3 |
| 1 small baked potato | 83 | 24 |
| 7 ounces fat-free yogurt | 24 | 3 |
| ½ cup bran cereal | 42 | 9 |
| 1 slice watermelon | 72 | 15 |
| 6 ounces orange juice | 57 | 11 |

Simple and low-fiber complex carbs can adversely affect health when consumed in inappropriate amounts. For example, overconsumption of these carbs for a number of years in genetically predisposed individuals can cause the pancreas to overproduce insulin. Insulin receptors then become resistant, causing excess sugar in the blood or hyperglycemia (type 2 diabetes). A large portion of this excess sugar is stored as fat, resulting in obesity. Too much insulin can also lead to atherosclerosis (hardening and narrowing of the arteries), heart disease, and hypertension.

While fiber is an important part of everyone's diet, carbohydrates in general are not. However, high-fiber complex carbs, such as those found in whole grains, should be consumed in proper amounts to maintain good health.

Sedentary lifestyles and genes can cause spikes in blood sugar levels that can promote insulin resistance. Eating more whole grains can improve this condition, although they must be consumed in appropriate amounts.

Include fruits, vegetables, and whole grain carbs each day. High-fiber vegetables, such as broccoli and lentils, are healthful choices for our nutritional needs. Intake of these foods is associated with a lower incidence of diabetes, arthritis, and numerous other diseases.

Good grains come from brown rice, whole grain pasta (such as whole rice pasta), quinoa, whole oats, and bulgur. They're loaded with vitamins, minerals, and other nutrients essential for good health. Carbs from these sources should provide the bulk of your daily calories.

Until recently, whole grain products were available only in health food stores. Today, however, supermarkets are carrying lines of these products. To add more grains to your daily regimen, begin with breakfast by eating cereals containing oats, barley, or other grains. Replace potatoes in your evening meal with brown rice or hulled barley. If you crave a macaroni dish, substitute whole rice spaghetti or organic brown rice.

These guidelines are for nondiabetic adults. If you are diabetic, consult with your physician regarding the foods you should eat.

## It's Your Choice

The purpose of my No Flour, No Sugar Diet is to allow overweight individuals to shed their fat with efficiency and safety and to promote long-term healthful eating habits. In the end, however, we make our own decisions about what to eat. I recommend that you stay up to date on nutritional studies and choose wisely.

# *The Skinny on Artificial Sweeteners*

Sugar substitutes are nonnutritive substances that provide little, if any, energy in the form of calories. They do not affect blood sugar levels and are intended to serve as an alternative to sugar. The Food and Drug Administration (FDA) approves sugar substitutes for use once they have been shown to be safe and effective. These products have been on the market for almost fifty years, with new brands being introduced on a regular basis. They reportedly help consumers lose weight and control diabetes. These sweeteners are often used for baking and in coffee, carbonated diet soft drinks, chewing gum, and a host of other products.

## A Nation of Sweet Consumers

The average American eats the equivalent of twenty teaspoons (almost three-fourths of a cup) of sugar each day! Nearly 60 percent of this intake is from high-calorie corn sweeteners (such as high-fructose corn syrup), which are used heavily in nearly all sweetened products such as sodas, juices, and frozen treats. Another 40 percent is from simple table sugar (sucrose), and a small amount comes from natural substances such as maple sugar or from molasses—the thick brown syrup produced in the process of refining raw sugar.

Experts agree there's nothing unusual about craving sweets. The problem results when the consumption of large quantities of sugars takes its toll, often resulting in excessive weight gain. One way the American population has countered this is through the use of sugar substitutes, and we are continually searching for good tasting, low-calorie products.

Yet, the use of sugar substitutes may actually trigger a craving for carbohydrates, increase appetite, and contribute to high-calorie consumption. If you choose to use sugar substitutes, stay within the acceptable daily intake (ADI)—levels that can be safely consumed every day.

The allowance of sugar substitutes in my No Flour, No Sugar Diet has been questioned by some people. Their concern is that these artificial substitutes may not be nutritious in the long run. This is a concern I understand. Yet my position is that many overweight people will be unsuccessful at dieting if they attempt to cut out all sweets. And, since there is no controversy over the severe health risks associated with being overweight, I suggest the use of FDA-approved sugar substitutes—within ADI levels—is an acceptable risk. My advice is to lose the weight first, then cut back on artificial sweeteners as best you can.

## Make Your Own Decision

The FDA evaluates sweeteners' compositions and properties before approving them. To date, five sugar substitutes have been approved by the FDA: aspartame, saccharin, sucralose, neotame, and acesulfame potassium. Because I believe people should have enough information to make their own informed decisions, below is a brief description of each.

### *Aspartame*

Brand names include Equal and NutraSweet.

Aspartame is converted in the body to methanol and two amino acids—aspartic acid and phenylalanine. It is almost two hundred times sweeter than sugar and is digested as a protein. Since the amounts used are minimal (within the ADI level), it is essentially calorie free. In 1981 it was first approved by the FDA as a sweetener for use in chewing gum, cereals, and other dry products. Its use expanded to soda in 1983 and then for use as a general-purpose sweetener in all foods and drinks in 1996.

This sweetener is reported to have a clean, sweet taste and does not promote tooth decay. It is currently found in more than six thousand products and is consumed by over two hundred million people around the world. It should be noted it has not been recommended for products that require prolonged exposure to high temperatures, as it loses its sweetness; however, an encapsulated form is now available for commercial baking. It can successfully be used in liquids but will lose its sweetness over an extended period of time.

Because of the phenylalanine component, aspartame does carry a risk for people with the rare genetic disorder known as phenylketonuria (PKU). Those who have this should restrict their intake of aspartame and adhere to package warning labels.

## Saccharin

Brand names include Sweet'N Low and Necta Sweet.

Saccharin was first discovered in 1879 and has been the subject of more than thirty studies in humans. Subsequently, it was introduced in 1957 as the first sugar substitute in powdered form. It is up to seven hundred times sweeter than sugar and has no calories. It is used in soft drinks, jams, chewing gum, tabletop sweeteners, and baked goods.

An interesting fact is that Benjamin Eisenstadt, its creator, was credited with inventing the sugar packet, and artificial sweetener packets were an outgrowth of that business.

## Sucralose

The brand name is Splenda.

Sucralose was first discovered thirty years ago. It is made from sugar through a manufacturing process that selectively replaces three atoms of chlorine for three hydroxyl groups on the sugar molecule. It should be noted that the chlorine used is *not* chlorine bleach. Chlorine is a naturally occurring atom present in foods such as lettuce and mushrooms. Sucralose is six hundred times sweeter than sugar and has no calories.

It was approved in 1998 for use in fifteen food categories—the broadest initial approval ever given to a food additive. Uses include tabletop sweeteners, in beverages, chewing gum, fruit juices, yogurt, applesauce, gelatins, frozen desserts, and more. Because it is so much sweeter than sugar, sucralose is bulked up with a flavorless starchy powder (maltodextrin) that allows it to be measured in a way similar to measuring sugar. It was approved as a general-purpose sweetener in all foods in 1999 and is currently used in more than four thousand products.

> *"I have lost eighty pounds on the No Flour, No Sugar Diet."*
>
> **Judy, Columbia City, Indiana**

Sucralose has been reported to be safe and effective for individuals with diabetes. Further, it has been reported to be safe as a food ingredient for the general population, including children and women who are pregnant or breast-feeding. Its safety in various categories is supported by more than one hundred studies conducted over a twenty-year period. There appear to be no known side effects. Sucralose is nontoxic and has been approved for use in more than eighty countries.

## Neotame

Neotame is up to thirteen thousand times sweeter than sugar and has no calories. In 2002 it was approved by the FDA as a general-purpose sweetener and is used in soft drinks, chewing gum, puddings, jams and jellies, toppings, frosting, syrups, and more. Neotame is structurally similar to aspartame and more than one hundred studies on animals and humans were conducted and reviewed by the FDA prior to approval.

### Acesulfame Potassium

Brand names for this product are Sunett and Sweet One.

Acesulfame potassium is two hundred times sweeter than sugar. It was first approved by the FDA in 1988 for specific uses—including tabletop sweeteners. Ten years later, it received approval for use in beverages, followed five years later for general use in foods—excluding meats and poultry. It is suggested for baking, as it retains its sweetness at normal baking temperatures.

Acesulfame potassium is made from a process that involves an organic intermediate, acetoacetic acid and potassium, to form a highly stable crystalline sweetener. It is not metabolized or stored in the body, therefore is calorie free.

It can be used by pregnant women and diabetics. Studies show that bacteria in the mouth do not metabolize this artificial sweetener. It does not convert into plaque or harmful acids. Thus, it does not contribute to tooth decay.

## Natural Sweeteners

If you are allergic to artificial sweeteners or simply prefer not to use them, there are several alternative choices.

Figs, dates, and raisins are excellent natural substitutes. A handful of one or a combination of them placed in a blender with a half cup of water and blended on low for a few minutes will produce a pudding-like mixture that is healthful and delicious. Try this in place of salad dressings, on hot cereal, and as a topping on fruit salad. You might even experiment using it as a sugar substitute in your baking.

Are you looking for something sweet on cold cereal? Simply chop dates or figs and sprinkle them over the cereal. You'll be pleasantly surprised.

Frozen fruit juice concentrates without added sugar are excellent for sweetening salad dressings. They're far more healthful than white sugar.

## Stevia

Stevia is derived from a South American shrub. It has the ability to sweeten foods yet does not have FDA approval in the United States because of laboratory findings that compounds in Stevia hold the *possibility* of changing genes. It is not known if this is likely to happen naturally.

Under 1994 legislation, Stevia can be sold as a dietary supplement but cannot be promoted as a sweetener.

Whatever you choose in the way of sweeteners, natural or otherwise, remember that moderation is the key to everything.

# 4

# The Place of Beverages in Your Diet

Have you been on a diet, or perhaps several diets over the years, and still can't seem to lose as much weight as you would like? Do you continue to wonder why, since you are carefully watching what you are eating, the pounds just hang in there? Maybe it isn't what you're eating, but what you're drinking. Let's review some possibilities and perhaps tighten up a bit.

## Gather the Information

Being conscious of exactly what you are eating and drinking is important when dieting. But, strange as it may seem, many of us don't have a clear idea of what we consume in a day. A good strategy is to keep a journal of what you eat and drink. For a week or so, write down everything consumed. It might be easy for you to remember that you had yogurt and an apple for breakfast, a chicken salad for lunch, and a prepared frozen entrée for dinner. But what about all the other things you nibbled on during the day? Did you chew a piece of gum or have a hard candy or two? Share a co-worker's bag of corn chips in the afternoon?

And, how about what you drank all day?

For example, did you have coffee with milk or sugar—or both milk and sugar—with breakfast? Did you and a friend walk over to the Starbucks across from your office for a midmorning latte? What did you drink with that salad at lunch? A soda with one free refill? Was a cold beer too tempting to ignore when you got home from work? And what about dinner? Another beer, perhaps a glass or two of wine? Iced tea with lemon and sugar?

Here are some thoughts on what you drink and how it might be affecting your dieting success or failure.

## Caffeine

The aroma of coffee is pleasurable; in fact, someone once pointed out to me it actually smells better than it tastes. Statistics reveal that 90 percent of all Americans consume caffeine every day in coffee, tea, chocolate, power and energy drinks, and enhanced waters.

Caffeine has been used for thousands of years to promote mental clarity and to help keep us awake. It also affects the central nervous system; can decrease conception rates; can cause insomnia, nervousness, and sweating; speeds up the pulse; and acts as a diuretic. Caffeine activates cortisol and the neurotransmitter dopamine, which in turn activates the pleasure center in the brain.

Too much coffee or caffeine consumed regularly can have an effect on attempted weight loss. An eight-ounce cup of black coffee contains zero calories and 100 milligrams of caffeine. One to two cups or up to 200 milligrams is considered safe for daily consumption. Research has shown that drinking more than two cups daily can raise blood sugar and affect the body's metabolism and its ability to burn fat. Sometimes decreasing your daily coffee consumption can have surprising results when you weigh in.

Another way it can affect your diet is that the half-life of caffeine in the body is up to six hours. This may explain that midday slump you sometimes experience. To get yourself out of this slump by eating a candy bar or other sugar- or flour-based snack will obviously adversely affect your diet's success. Remember also that caffeine is present in chocolate. Of course, if you are a devotee of my No Flour, No Sugar Diet, you wouldn't be eating that candy bar anyway, so give yourself a well-deserved pat on the back.

## Juices

Did you forget about the glass of juice you have every morning with your vitamins? Eight ounces of orange juice contains 110 calories. This is not to imply you should eliminate this healthful drink from your diet. But consider this: if you are a person who needs to consume a daily average of 2,000 calories to maintain your desired weight, one glass of orange juice is about 5 percent of your daily allotment of calories. Eliminating 5 percent of your caloric intake here and 5 percent there, even from the foods allowed in my No Flour, No Sugar Diet, is a good strategy for losing weight quickly. And all "juices" aren't created equal. Many juices on the market contain only 10 percent juice. Read labels to determine the percentage of juice content—as opposed to the sugar content. Choose appropriately.

## Teas

Do you have a pick-me-up cup of tea once the hectic beginning of the morning settles down? This is a wise choice, as teas have no calories. Studies reveal the flavonoids in white and green teas appear to be extremely effective antioxidants, helping neutralize free radicals that can lead to some cancers. Other studies reveal that tea drinkers have a reduced incidence of cancer of the breast, lung, skin, and mouth. Black tea contains 50 milligrams of caffeine, half that of coffee. Decaffeinated teas contain only 4 milligrams of caffeine, and herbal forms are completely caffeine free.

We have long heard of the benefits of green tea. A recent study by Japanese scientists indicates early-stage breast cancer spreads less rapidly in women with a history of drinking five or more cups of green tea daily. Green tea is also free of calories, with each tea bag containing approximately 130 milligrams of flavonoid antioxidants. The alluring aroma is often just the right touch for a pick-me-up.

When you're buying bottled tea at the store, check the label carefully. Bottled teas with sugar added contain about 100 calories per serving. Should you buy and drink a sixteen-ounce bottle, you will have consumed 200 calories. Why? Because a sixteen-ounce bottle is considered to have two servings.

With the wide range of herbal teas available, there is virtually something for everyone. Experiment with brewing your own and then try your favorite over ice.

## Alcohol

Beverages containing alcohol do not contain fat, nor do they supply any appreciable amount of nutrients. Generally speaking, they are high in calories. Consider that 12 ounces of beer contain 150 calories, 1½ ounces of brandy contain 135 calories, 1½ ounces of vodka 105 calories, and 5 ounces of wine up to 120 calories.

Recent studies have shown that daily consumption of moderate amounts of alcohol—one drink or glass of wine a day for women, two for men—has a positive effect on a person's longevity. Red wine is said to be especially beneficial (as is purple grape juice).

Yet, nutritional deficiencies can occur in heavy drinkers for a variety of reasons. One is that consumption of nutritious foods is often replaced by the alcohol. Also, the consumption of these beverages reduces the absorption of some vitamins. For example, alcohol abuse is the most common cause of thiamin ($B_1$) deficiency in the Western world. This water-soluble vitamin keeps the heart and nervous systems functioning properly and joins with pyruvic acid to aid the breakdown of carbohydrates into glucose.

Excessive alcohol is also a common cause of low magnesium, resulting from poor diet and increased urinary and fecal loss. Magnesium is important for nerves and muscles.

Therefore, if you are attempting to eat a nutrient-rich, healthful diet, lose weight, or maintain your current weight, moderating your intake of alcohol-containing beverages is appropriate.

## Water

And now, the best for last. Water, the most essential liquid you can consume, is completely without calories and makes up about 60 percent of your body weight. It serves to keep your joints lubricated and your temperature regulated, and it provides the fluid required to process thousands of your normal bodily functions.

Today's consumer is overwhelmed with the availability of bottled water. There are many brands to choose from, with some imported from faraway lands.

You've probably also noticed the recent influx of no-calorie, flavored water beverages on the market today. Some are sweetened with Splenda. These drinks are exactly what they say—flavored water. If you find you are having trouble drinking enough water because of the taste, or lack thereof, you may want to try some of these. Drinking them will not only increase your water intake, but when they replace sweetened drinks your daily calorie consumption will be reduced.

A new type of bottled water called "fitness water" may not contain calories; however, many varieties of it are heavily loaded with caffeine. What's more, that caffeine content is often not listed on the label. Be aware of this if you are trying to limit your caffeine intake.

Truth be told, bottled water is a multibillion-dollar industry that provides exactly the same product your kitchen faucet does. If you prefer ice-cold water, leave a filled container in your refrigerator. For a special dinner, serve water in wineglasses, with the rim of each glass rubbed with a lemon or lime slice. Then drop the slice in the water with an ice cube or two and enjoy the delightful, refreshing flavor. By the way—the calorie count? Zero.

Drinking water, tea, and other beverages is good for you. It's the drinks with added sugars and other "enhancements" that are the culprits. The next time you pick up a can or bottle, read the label. You might be quite surprised at what you find.

## 5

# *Avoiding the Yo-yo Effect*

frequently hear from readers who tell me that, over the years, they have tried one diet or another and lost ten, twenty, thirty or more pounds, only to put them back on in subsequent months. Then they repeat the whole process. Weight up. Weight down. Weight up. Weight down. Like a yo-yo. As a matter of fact that's just what it is called: yo-yo dieting. This is a very common pattern among dieters. We often come to the brilliant realization it is time to go on a diet when our clothes don't fit the way they did a few months earlier, or when we know summer is coming and it will be shorts and bathing suit weather soon. We jump on the diet wagon, lose enough weight to get into whatever it is we couldn't, then gain the weight back. This often leads to a feeling of discouragement and a permanent return to the pattern of eating that created the weight problem in the first place. Of course, we should have made the decision to catch our weight gain months or years earlier when we had only a few pounds to drop. Now we're looking at twenty-five or thirty pounds—maybe even more—and we are impatient. What can we do to get the immediate results we crave?

Keep in mind that crash diets are just that. They're unrealistic and you simply "crash" under the pressure. Extreme diets are incredibly difficult to stick with. You feel restricted, hungry, and cheated, and you blame the diet plan. You may go off the selected diet for several days, weeks, or months and, you guessed it, eventually gain back at least all of the lost weight, if not more. This unfortunate situation is a common consequence of many diet plans. Not only is this phenomenon frustrating, it is unhealthful.

You do have options. My No Flour, No Sugar Diet is flexible, easy to understand, easy to follow, and easy to stay on; hence it does not lead to a yo-yo effect. It's a workable plan that helps people achieve weight-loss goals that are consistent and lasting—just the opposite of the yo-yo pattern.

Impossible, you say? Think again. I have received tens of thousands of letters from people who have tried every diet available. The restrictions in those diet plans prevent them from keeping unwanted weight off. They're constantly amazed at how simple my program is. Further, it works for people of every age and you don't walk around hungry all the time. There are no restrictions, other than to avoid flour and added sugar.

So, if you really want to impress people when you show up at the beach or attend the annual Black & White Formal, don't wait. Let's get you started now on the right track. Begin by asking yourself if you have realistic goals for a weight-loss program. Keep in mind that a reduction of ten pounds for one person can be as dramatic and grueling as fifty or sixty for another. All excess weight is difficult to drop.

A reasonable and healthy goal is to lose one to two pounds a week. By eliminating all flour and added sugar from your diet, you might lose four, five, or more pounds the first week. Then you might experience a slump where you remain stable or lose less than your desired amount. Don't get discouraged. Just stick to the plan: no flour, no sugar. In the long run, you will keep those pounds off and continue to lose by modifying your eating habits in ways that will become second nature to you.

There will probably be occasions when you deviate from the No Flour, No Sugar Diet. This is expected. Don't berate yourself, just start up again immediately. As a matter of fact, wandering off the diet

a bit is even encouraged in some instances, such as when you are cel-
ebrating holidays or on vacation. Just don't make it a permanent habit.
It is best if you plan in advance for these departures by eating smaller
portions than normal, cutting out your daily glass of wine, or doing
something else that lowers your caloric intake for a week or two beforehand. You might find by doing this, you end up with a greater net
weight loss for the period than had you not planned to go off the diet.

# 6

# Dealing with Special Events

Everybody loves a party but dieters know that it can ruin weight management plans. Special events, including holidays, birthdays, weddings, and graduations, can present hard-to-resist opportunities to interrupt dieting. We all know that if we attend a party, we will be offered—and will most likely accept—foods we shouldn't be eating.

Somehow, puff pastries filled with gooey cheeses, cakes with luscious frostings, brownies with caramel swirls, little hot dogs in rolled pastry dough, deep-fried shrimp, and countless other calorie-laden dishes always end up being the menu du jour. And the temptation to munch on them can be nearly overwhelming. After all, we tell ourselves, they look so good and they're so small. Maybe the calories won't rack up all that quickly. And it's only for this one evening.

Does this rationalizing sound familiar? If it does, and staying on your diet at special events has been a problem for you in the past, I'm happy to report that occasional cheating in these situations is acceptable on my No Flour, No Sugar Diet—with caveats.

## Forewarned Is Forearmed

Christmas, birthdays, New Year's Eve parties, and other holidays and special events are entirely predictable. You know they're coming. The July Fourth picnic bash and your best friend's birthday don't arrive unheralded. You know the baked beans, sesame-seeded hamburger buns, ice cream, cherry pie, and so much more will be awaiting you on the table. And remember the taste of your best friend's Mexican casserole from last year when, incidentally, you weighed less than you do now? You had three helpings. Well, she's bringing a duplicate this year. You decide you'll never be thin again.

Okay, enough of that. You know what's coming, so now it's time to take some preemptive steps to protect the progress you've made on your diet.

1. Weigh yourself and write down the result. Plan to weigh yourself three or four days after the event to see how you've fared. Knowing where you stand and knowing you are going to be checking up on yourself will help supply the motivation you'll need to eat better during the event.

2. Cut down on what you eat for a week or two in advance of the event. Plan lighter meals, back away from the table a little sooner, decline a second glass of wine with dinner, or find some other small way to lower your calorie intake. You will see an increase in your weight reduction and thus will have a little more flexibility when the get-together is upon you.

3. Exercise more for a week prior to the event. You'd be surprised what five to ten more minutes on the stair-climber or adding another half mile to your daily walk can do for you. Not only are you working off calories, but you are also increasing the body's production of endorphins, the biochemical compounds that promote a feeling of well-being. This is likely to help you deal with any feelings of deprivation you may experience when declining that piece of chocolate cake.

Keep in mind it is okay to gain a pound or two. You have not failed at dieting.

## Don't Keep Your Diet a Secret

You may not want to make a public announcement that you are on a diet as soon as you arrive, but quietly letting those who keep offering you fattening foods know that you are on a diet and have trouble with temptation is usually sufficient to make them cease. This shouldn't embarrass you. Taking care of your health is something of which to be proud. More than one person in the crowd will be envious of your willpower.

## Alcohol

Alcohol is one source of empty calories that you can avoid, but what about the pressures of joining the fun? You've just entered the room and everyone has a drink in hand. The punch on the table has floating sherbet added for color and flavor. It certainly looks good, but you know it contains lots of sugar. There's a full bar across the room and you can see open wine bottles on a table next to it. What should you do?

My No Flour, No Sugar Diet allows alcohol consumption, but remember that common sense and moderation are called for. Even two or three drinks during a four-hour evening can really rack up the calories. So what can you do and still join the party? Ask for a glass of club soda with a lemon twist or a squeeze of lime. Drink diet soft drinks. Ask if they have sugar-free iced tea, or reach for a bottle of spring water. There are likely to be numerous choices available.

If you would like to enjoy a drink or a glass of wine, sandwich it in between nonalcoholic drinks.

## Nibbles

Believe it or not, most parties offer plenty of healthful food choices. Is there a brightly colored vegetable platter with broccoli florets, red peppers, carrot sticks, raw mushrooms, and more? Is it placed next to a plate of deep-fried breaded cheese sticks? Which one should you choose? This is a no-brainer.

Is someone passing around little hot dogs wrapped in rolls, deep-fried mushrooms, cheese puffs, and other fattening things? Don't feel deprived. Simply smile and indicate that the vegetables are so appealing you have to say no to the other hors d'oeuvres.

If the party includes a full meal, it is likely that there will be plenty of healthful choices. This is especially true if the meal is served buffet style. Most buffets have more than one meat choice and a number of salad and vegetable choices. Choose the leanest meat and load up on the vegetables and salads.

If it is a sit-down dinner where you haven't a choice of servings, eat only the portions that fit the No Flour, No Sugar Diet. You'll usually find you'll still have plenty to eat.

Of course, if you are the one throwing the party, just use the recipes in this book and surprise everyone with how good no-flour, no-sugar eating really is.

## And Finally, Indulge a Little

Life is too short not to indulge a bit. Yes, it is all right to have a bite of strawberry cheesecake or a few fried mushrooms. That's what I meant when I said occasional cheating is allowed on my diet. Just keep your head and don't overdo it.

# 7

# Some Surprising Calorie Contents

Calories are in nearly every food we eat. So what is a calorie, anyway? Simply put, it's another word for energy. Our bodies use calories from the food we eat as energy for everything we do, from playing soccer to thinking. Each of us, the thinnest to the most obese, has fat cells, and this is where unused calories are stored. They remain there until the body needs them, at which time they are turned into energy and burned through activity.

Some of us are very active and burn more calories per hour or per day than those of us who spend our time sitting in a chair or on the couch. It stands to reason that a child playing baseball on a field will burn more calories than will an older person watching a television program. Since we usually quit running around as we did when we were children, we naturally gain weight as we age. Our sedentary lifestyles cause us to bulk up more.

But keeping active and fit helps us to keep trim in another rather amazing way. Muscle tissue burns more calories at rest than does fatty tissue. Therefore a 250-pound man in good shape expends more calories sitting on a couch than a 250-pound out-of-shape individual sitting on the same couch whose weight comes from fat rather than from muscle. This means the better shape you get in, the easier it will be to stay at your desired weight.

The number of calories you need changes as your lifestyle changes. We tend to spend more time at home during winter months than we would in warmer weather. It's more difficult to get exercise inside your house, whereas you might work in the yard, walk around the block, or do other activities outdoors. As a result, we often put on a few extra pounds over the winter, which becomes evident when we can't fit into spring or summer clothing.

The FDA uses a 2,000-calorie diet as the basis for calculating the daily values that appear on food labels. But not everyone requires the same number of calories each day. Determinations for the amount per day include body size, activity level, height, weight, age, and more. Since each person is different, it is important for you to know your own needs in terms of calories. Smaller, more sedentary people need fewer calories than larger, more active people.

You can calculate a very rough estimate of how many calories you need to eat daily to maintain your current weight from the formulas that follow.

If you are sedentary: multiply your weight times 11.
If you are moderately active: multiply your weight times 13.
If you are active: multiply your weight times 15.

The answer you get is the approximate number of calories your body needs if you plan to keep your weight at its present level. Let me reemphasize that this gives you only a rough estimate.

## No Calorie Counting Necessary

On my No Flour, No Sugar Diet, I don't require calorie counting. You will lose extra weight simply by cutting out flour and sugar. But knowledge is power, and if you understand the basics of calories, read food labels when buying processed foods, and choose to eat foods that are lower in calories, you will speed along the progress of your diet. Since one pound of fat is roughly equal to 3,500 calories, to lose one pound a week, you must reduce your calorie consumption by 500 calories each day. Using the formula above, let's say you weigh 180 pounds and are moderately active. The rough number of calories your body needs to maintain that 180 pounds is 2,340 (180 x 13 = 2,340). To lose one pound a week you would need to cut your calories down to 1,840 a day.

A word of caution is called for here. Even when you are dieting, your caloric intake shouldn't go below 1,200 a day. You need at least that many calories—derived from nutritious, well-balanced foods—to maintain your body's general health.

## Limit Fat

For a number of health reasons, no more than 30 percent of your calorie intake should come from fat. Because the values on food labels for fats and other nutritional items are based on a 2,000-calorie diet, these label recommendations are only a starting point. However, if you ingest 2,000 calories each day, your limit for fat calories is 600. This translates to no more than 65 grams of fat a day.

> *"I've always had a problem with my weight and diets never worked for me. I would gain back the weight as soon as I went off the diet. When I started Dr. Gott's No Flour, No Sugar Diet, I weighed 194 pounds. I am now at 146 pounds. I feel great! Thank you for your wonderful advice."*
>
> *Veronica, Clovis, California*

## Quicker Than You Think

Okay, so how *do* those calories add up so quickly? What about the few wheat crackers you snack on during the day? To begin with, they're made of enriched flour, whole grain wheat flour, sugar, high-fructose corn syrup, and more. No wonder they taste so good. The downside is that each tiny cracker contains almost 17 calories and there are 6 grams of fat in a normal serving of just nine crackers.

Do you enjoy dunking biscotti into your coffee or tea? Biscotti are made with enriched wheat flour, unbleached flour, malted barley flour, and sugar. A single serving contains 140 calories, 45 fat calories, and 5 grams of total fat. This doesn't seem like such a good choice anymore, does it?

And how about a candy bar, the delectable temptation you encounter next to most supermarket checkout stands? One two-ounce bar delivers about 280 calories, 130 of them from fat.

Take a look at the calorie list in table 7.1; there may be some surprises for you.

**TABLE 7.1**

| Food | Calories |
|------|----------|
| Apple pie, homemade, ⅛ pie | 411 |
| Applesauce, sweetened, 1 cup | 195 |
| Bacon, cooked, 1 ounce | 163 |
| Bagel, plain | 245 |
| Baked beans with franks, canned, 1 cup | 368 |
| Beer, 12 ounces | 150 |
| Biscuit, buttermilk, homemade, 4" round | 358 |
| Bread, white, 1 slice | 80 |
| Butter, 4 tablespoons | 405 |
| Cheese, American, 1 ounce | 106 |
| Cheese, whole milk ricotta, ¼ cup | 107 |
| Chicken pot pie, small, frozen | 484 |
| Chocolate cake, homemade, no frosting, ⅛ cake | 340 |

| Food | Calories |
|------|----------|
| Chocolate éclair | 250 |
| Coffee cake, 1½" square | 100 |
| Cola, 12 ounces | 160 |
| Cream, heavy whipping, 1 tablespoon | 52 |
| Danish pastry with fruit | 263 |
| Doughnut, plain cake | 210 |
| Egg, fried | 120 |
| Eggnog, 1 cup | 343 |
| French toast, 2 slices, with butter | 356 |
| Hot chocolate made with milk, 8 ounces | 180 |
| Juice drink, 8 ounces | 120 |
| Nuts, oil-roasted peanuts or cashews, 1 ounce | 163 |
| Onion rings, frozen, 10 | 244 |
| Potato chips, 20 | 210 |
| Potatoes au gratin with butter, homemade, 1 cup | 323 |
| Raisins, ¼ cup | 108 |
| Rice, long grain white, cooked, 1 cup | 225 |
| Sausage link, 2.4 ounces | 229 |
| Steak, sirloin, lean, trimmed, 8 ounces | 496 |
| Strawberry ice cream, ½ cup | 230 |
| Trail mix with nuts, chocolate chips, seeds, 1 cup | 707 |
| Vanilla custard, ⅔ cup | 200 |
| Waffle, plain | 215 |

| Fast Food | Calories |
|---|---|
| Chicken fillet sandwich, plain | 515 |
| Chocolate malt, medium | 600 |
| Fish sandwich with tartar sauce and cheese | 523 |
| French fries, regular size | 220 |
| French toast, 5 slices | 513 |
| Fried chicken, 1 thigh and 1 breast | 629 |
| Hamburger, ¼ pound, with cheese | 524 |

These caloric contents will vary, depending on the product you purchase, the way it is prepared, and what is added, both at the food-processing plant and at home. Nonetheless, you can easily see that some foods you might consider nutritious and healthful in a daily diet may not be.

It's difficult attempting to get or stay lean in our society. Food is available everywhere, at any time, and, it seems, the Great American Pastime is no longer baseball, but eating.

Calories are necessary, but it is often hard to pick the right ones. You are bombarded daily with an abundance of poor yet tasty food choices and this makes it extremely easy for you to overindulge. But you can be in control. You can make intelligent choices, and, pretty soon, bypassing chocolate chip cookies for fresh fruit will be commonplace for you. If you stay focused, you can do anything, including sticking to my No Flour, No Sugar Diet and maintaining a healthy weight.

## 8

# *Stocking the Larder*

The foods you pick to stock in your home and the quantities you choose to have on hand have a major impact on the success or failure of your diet.

As you know, a great deal of what many of us end up eating are foods full of empty calories. This is so because these foods are easily accessible as we go through our day and we succumb to their temptations. To fight this easy availability is tough enough at work, at friends' homes, or when you eat out, but it is especially difficult when you open your own pantry or refrigerator and find it stocked with the same poor choices. Good choices are made easier when you always have the right types of foods in your kitchen. Here are a number I would suggest as staples.

## Plain Yogurt

Many of the dishes in this book call for plain yogurt. This versatile dairy product can be used in dips for raw vegetables, as part of a dessert, or over baked potatoes in place of sour cream.

## Olive Oil and Cooking Sprays

You'll notice that extra virgin olive oil is used in many of my recipes. It can be used to sauté and as an ingredient in salad dressings, in homemade granola bars, and in a host of other dishes. I prefer this to other oils because it will not raise your blood cholesterol level—important for good cardiovascular health—and it imparts a pleasing flavor to nearly any dish.

Cooking sprays have been around since the 1950s and have become a kitchen mainstay. They are easy to use and often provide fewer calories and fats because the spray allows for a thinner coating. They are often made from a combination of oils. You can make your own from your preferred oil (or oils) by placing it in a spray bottle, such as a plant mister. Be sure the bottle is new and washed with hot, soapy water before you use it.

## Jam Made of 100 Percent Fruit

You'll find that I mention Simply Fruit brand fruit preserves in some recipes. This isn't because I own stock in the company, but because it is made of 100 percent fruit and it is widely available. There are other similar brands out there, just check labels to make sure there's no added sugar. These jams are useful as a glaze over pork chops, spread over warmed Brie, combined with sugar-free mustard for a sweet-and-sour sauce, and more.

## Sugar-Free Peanut Butter

Sugar-free peanut butter is another good staple. It can be used in numerous snack and cookie recipes and is full of protein.

## Dates and Figs

Dates and figs, two fruits you probably don't consider purchasing on a regular basis—if at all—are called for in several of my recipes.

They contain natural sugars that take the place of table sugar. These natural sweeteners are excellent in fruit and nut bars and in trail mix recipes. Try homemade Figgy Date Syrup over hot cereal.

## Tea

Green and white teas are full of nutrients, free of calories, and essential in my cupboard. I heartily endorse them for yours. Try having a cup of herbal, green, or white tea when you think you are hungry. You might be pleasantly surprised by the results.

## Ground Turkey and Ground Chicken

Ground turkey and ground chicken are available in one-pound sleeves that can be popped into your freezer to have on hand for future use. These lean products are a good substitute for other cuts of meat or poultry with a high fat content. Ground chicken is more moist, making it good for hamburger patties, while ground turkey is slightly drier and goes well with sauces, such as tomato sauce served over whole rice pasta.

## Rolled Oats

Quick-cooking rolled oats take the place of flour in many recipes in this book. It's quite surprising to realize cookies, granola bars, and so much more can be made without flour. Have fun experimenting with this versatile, inexpensive food. And don't forget how quick, warming, and filling it is for breakfast.

## Flourless Bread

Stock at least one loaf of bread—yes, you read right—bread. Sprouted whole wheat berry breads are made without flour, sugar, or oil. Instead, they're baked with organic dates, raisins, and other nutri-ent-rich ingredients. What could be better?

Keep a sliced loaf in your freezer. When you want a piece of toast for breakfast or a sugar-free peanut butter snack, remove the loaf from the freezer, carefully insert a knife between the slices and break away as many as you need. Pop them frozen in your toaster and return the remainder to your freezer.

## Veggies

Vegetables are a boon to your health, providing nutrients and fiber. Stock peppers, squashes, broccoli, bok choy, celery, lettuce, radishes, and cauliflower—the list can go on and be nearly endless. Purchase vegetables by the week and store them washed and cut into easy-to-use pieces in your refrigerator. Most grocery stores vary their produce selections by the season. Each time you go to replenish your supply, see what new veggies are available and give them a try.

## Fruit

Fruit is always a good choice. Remember when you purchase fruit to select some at varying degrees of ripeness. Buying a few pieces that are slightly green will allow you to eat some toward the end of the week. This is especially true of bananas. Most fruit does well when stored in your refrigerator. If you find your fruit is ripening too quickly, and you fear you won't have time to eat it all, pop it into your refrigerator for another day.

## Nuts

Dry-roasted almonds and other nuts are healthful and filling. Many of my recipes have a variety of nuts as an ingredient. If they are read-ily available in a canister or bowl, they'll keep you from considering another empty-calorie choice.

Select healthful, no flour, no sugar staples you and your family will enjoy, ones you will eat on a regular basis. It is important to have plenty of variety on hand at all times so you can always be satisfied.

### Dealing with Food Labels

It is important to read labels when you're purchasing food. I constantly receive letters that include packaging labels asking if a particular food item is acceptable. Oftentimes, people are confused because the nutrition facts label indicates the item has X grams of sugar. Nutrition facts labels include naturally occurring sugars as well as added sugars. To ensure that a food or drink is okay to consume while on my diet, check the ingredients list on the package for specifics. If it lists sugar, high-fructose corn syrup, or other types of added sugar, then the food is not allowed. You might be surprised to find that unexpected foods like ketchup and fruit-flavored yogurt do contain added sugar. Please keep in mind that foods such as milk, 100 percent fruit juice, and vegetables all contain natural sugars. These items are allowed and encouraged on my diet.

# Part II

*The No Flour, No Sugar Recipes*

# 9

## *Breakfast*

I would venture to guess that very few Americans wake up in the morning and take the time to prepare themselves and their families a nourishing breakfast. We often oversleep and have twenty things to do before launching ourselves out the front door. We all know it's difficult to set aside enough time for a well-balanced start to the morning. Of course many people wouldn't want to—even if time allowed. They are too hooked on sugary breakfast cereals, toaster tarts, microwave waffles drenched in syrup, and other unhealthful foods. And, well, there's always that doughnut shop on the corner near the bus stop or the vending machine at the office. Just grab that cup of joe and run.

### Don't Skip Breakfast to Lose Weight

Some people skip breakfast as a way to lose weight. The idea is "If I don't eat breakfast, it's just that many fewer calories I'll consume during the day." But skipping breakfast doesn't actually help people maintain a healthy weight. In fact, someone who skips breakfast tends to eat more calories throughout the day.

The National Weight Control Registry, an organization that maintains a database of more than five thousand people who have lost at least thirty pounds and kept the weight off for at least one year, reports finding that eating breakfast every day was a weight control strategy for 78 percent of the people in the registry. These "experts" at weight control are onto something.

Studies prove that skipping breakfast leads to a feeling of fatigue and loss of energy at midmorning. Still other studies show that eating breakfast is important in maintaining health. Besides staying slimmer, breakfast eaters are more mentally alert and may even live longer.

A breakfast high in such things as whole grains and fruit will give you the physical and mental energy to have an enjoyable and successful morning. Instead of being tempted to fill up on high-calorie, high-fat foods for a midmorning pick-me-up, you'll be more likely to choose a piece of fruit or other sensible snack. Or even make it to lunch without snacking.

## Keep It Simple

I've included some wonderful quick and easy-to-prepare breakfast recipes in this chapter, but still simpler breakfast strategies exist for those days when you are truly time challenged. These include wheat farina, an instant hot breakfast cereal that can be purchased at your local grocery store. All you have to do is tear open an individual serving packet, pour it into a bowl, and mix in enough hot water to blend. Or you can try the old standby rolled oats for a filling breakfast. Oatmeal made from 100 percent rolled oats is a great way to add fiber to your diet, as well as being delicious. And what could be simpler than putting ½ cup of oats in a bowl with 1 cup of water and heating them for 3 minutes?

As a topping for either of these hot cereals, you can add raisins, chopped dates, or chopped figs. Or, see page 54 for a sweet topping that can easily be made with natural ingredients. A couple of spoonfuls of this tasty, puddinglike blend warmed in the microwave and drizzled over your hot cereal make a healthful, delicious dish. That's definitely acceptable in anyone's hectic day.

For a quicker alternative to hot cereal, consider shredded wheat, made from 100 percent whole wheat, with skim milk. And you can put the above toppings on it. If you're really on the run, a serving of low-fat, plain yogurt and a piece of fruit make an excellent breakfast.

## Plan Ahead

A breakfast dish assembled the evening before or over the weekend takes the pressure off morning preparation. Make it when time permits and freeze in serving-size packages as a way of relieving early morning stress. For example, you could pop a frozen Banana Oat Muffin into the microwave for fifteen seconds or so to heat thoroughly. Then fix a small side bowl of cut fruit such as a banana, an apple, or a pineapple-grape medley. The end result will be a nutritious, colorful, and enjoyable breakfast. Prepared in advance, a nutritious meal awaits you within a matter of minutes.

## Start Your Day Right

Breakfasts should be enjoyable and stress free. Furthermore, eating a nutrient-rich breakfast will make you feel good all day long. So set your alarm clock as little as ten minutes earlier. This will allow you time to start the coffee, warm a muffin you made last weekend, stick a bowl of oatmeal in the microwave, or munch on an apple and still make it to work on time. You're already on your way toward a better day!

# Country Breakfast Casserole

*Peggy Krueger, Abilene, Kansas*

Hash browns add a delightful flavor to this dish and ensure that you won't walk away hungry.

½ small green pepper, chopped
½ small onion, chopped
1 tablespoon butter
24 ounces frozen hash browns, thawed
9 eggs
Cooking spray, for coating
6 strips bacon, fried and crumbled
¼ cup nonfat milk
8 ounces cheddar cheese, shredded
Salt and black pepper to taste

Preheat oven to 350 degrees.

Sauté pepper and onion in butter. Add hash browns and 1 beaten egg. Pat into a 9" x 13" baking dish coated with cooking spray. Bake 20 minutes. While hash browns are baking, blend remaining eggs, bacon, and milk in bowl. Scramble mixture and fold in cheese. Spread mixture over top of baked hash browns once they come from oven. Season with salt and pepper. Return dish to oven and heat another 10 minutes. Serve.

Variation: Top with picante sauce.

*Serves 6 to 8*

# Banana Nut Muesli

*Patti Deinhardt, Yardville, New Jersey*

Here's a recipe to prepare in the evening, when you might have a little more time. Simply pull it out of the refrigerator in the morning and add warm milk for a taste-tempting start to the day.

⅔ cup rolled oats
1 firm banana, sliced
¼ cup raisins
¼ cup nuts, chopped
1 cup water
¼ teaspoon ground cinnamon

Mix all ingredients in bowl. Cover and refrigerate overnight. Serve with warm milk.

*Serves 2*

# Banana Oat Muffins

*Rosemarie McCoach, Sellersville, Pennsylvania*

These muffins combine the homey flavor of bananas with blueberries. Enjoy the results.

Cooking spray, for coating
2 cups oat bran
¼ cup old-fashioned rolled oats
2½ teaspoons baking powder
¼ teaspoon salt
¼ teaspoon ground cinnamon
Dash of ground nutmeg
2 ripe bananas, mashed
2 eggs, lightly beaten
½ cup soy milk
2 tablespoons extra virgin olive oil
½ teaspoon vanilla extract
½ cup nuts, chopped
1 cup blueberries

Preheat oven to 400 degrees.

Coat 12 muffin cups with cooking spray or use baking cups.

In large bowl, combine oat bran, rolled oats, baking powder, salt, cinnamon, and nutmeg.

In small bowl, beat together bananas, eggs, milk, oil, and vanilla. Stir liquid ingredients into dry ingredients until just blended. Then fold in nuts and blueberries. Divide batter into the muffin cups. Bake 18 to 23 minutes, or until toothpick inserted into center comes out clean. Serve warm or cold.

*Makes 12 muffins*

# Tastes Like Cookie Dough Oatmeal

*Cheryl Henderhan, Trinway, Ohio*

This tastes just like oatmeal cookie dough. Leftovers can even been eaten cold straight from the fridge. For variety, sprinkle with nuts and raisins.

1 stick butter, softened
1 cup granular Splenda
2 eggs
2 teaspoons baking powder
1 teaspoon salt
5 teaspoons (or to taste) ground cinnamon
2 cups milk
3 cups old-fashioned rolled oats

In large glass microwave-safe bowl, cream butter and Splenda with electric mixer. Add eggs and beat again. Then add baking powder, salt, and cinnamon. Mix 1 minute longer. Slowly add milk until mixed. Add oats, 1 cup at a time, mixing after each addition. Cover bowl (I use a dinner plate) and cook in microwave 4 minutes on high. Stir and continue cooking, covered, on 50 percent power 6 minutes. Serve.

*Serves 6*

# Breakfast Frittatas

What a great way to start the morning. This dish is full of tempting ingredients that are sure to please. To give it a spicier flavor, replace the red bell pepper with a teaspoon of crushed red pepper flakes or add a half teaspoon of chopped jalapeño.

Cooking spray, for coating
1 cup egg substitute
4 tablespoons chopped fresh spinach
2 tablespoons chopped red bell pepper
8 fresh button mushrooms, sliced
2 teaspoons chopped fresh chives
4 grape tomatoes, halved
2 ounces low-fat mozzarella cheese, shredded
Salt and black pepper to taste

Coat two 3-cup microwave-safe bowls with cooking spray. Combine all ingredients and divide into bowls. Microwave each bowl separately on high about 2 minutes, or until mixture has risen up and appears solid. If additional cooking time is required, microwave in 10-second increments. Slide frittatas onto plates and serve.

*Serves 2*

# Faux French Toast

Here's another breakfast dish that is easily prepared in advance. It has all the characteristics of French toast, without the flour and sugar, and is a refreshing change.

3 cups water
3 individual packets Splenda
½ teaspoon salt
2 teaspoons ground cinnamon
2 cups rolled oats
Cooking spray, for coating
1 cup Figgy Date Syrup or chopped fresh fruit, for topping

On stovetop, in medium-size pot, bring water, Splenda, salt, and cinnamon to a boil. Stir in oats. Cook 3 to 4 minutes over medium heat. Remove from heat and cover. Let stand about 5 minutes.

Coat 4" x 8" loaf pan with cooking spray. Pour mixture into pan and smooth with spoon. Cover and refrigerate overnight. When you're ready to cook, run knife around edges of pan to unmold. Cut into slices the thickness of bread. Fry on griddle or in frying pan coated with cooking spray until golden brown. Top with syrup and serve.

*Serves 4*

# Figgy Date Syrup

This delectable syrup can be used over Faux French Toast, or on anything that needs a touch of sweetness.

½ cup sugar-free pitted dried whole dates
½ cup sugar-free dried whole figs
½ cup warm water

Check figs and dates to ensure all stems and pits are removed. Place in blender and add ¼ cup water. Blend, adding remaining water if mixture is too thick. It should have a rich dark brown syrupy texture when done. If you want thinner syrup, simply add more warm water until you get the desired consistency.

*Makes 1½ cups*

# Oat Bran

This warm breakfast dish is easy enough to prepare and is full of crunchy walnuts. It's a winner for tasting good and taking just a few minutes to prepare.

½ cup oat bran
1 teaspoon ground cinnamon
4 tablespoons walnuts, chopped
2 tablespoons chopped dates or raisins
1 apple, cored, peeled, and diced
2 cups water
Dash of salt
½ cup nonfat milk

Combine all ingredients in microwave-safe bowl. Heat on high 5 minutes. Remove from microwave. Spoon into 2 bowls and pour skim milk over top before serving.

*Serves 2*

# Spicy Scrambled Eggs

This dish is sure to get you going first thing in the morning.

2 eggs, beaten
½ cup shredded cheddar cheese
1 scallion, chopped
½ jalapeño pepper, seeded and diced
½ cup diced ham
Salt and black pepper to taste
Cooking spray, for coating

Combine all ingredients in bowl. Pour into frying pan coated with cooking spray. Fold gently with spatula until eggs are fully cooked and veggies are tender. Serve with fresh fruit, if desired.

*Serves 2*

# Banana Muffins

These muffins are easy to make and freeze well. Place them in individual serving packages in your freezer and microwave for fifteen seconds for breakfast.

4 cups oatmeal
1 cup unsweetened applesauce
8 egg whites, whipped until foamy
6 bananas, mashed
2 cups Splenda
1½ teaspoons vanilla extract
2 teaspoons baking soda
2 teaspoons ground cinnamon
10 tablespoons soy milk
1 teaspoon butter
Cooking spray, for coating

Preheat oven to 350 degrees.

Combine all ingredients in bowl. Pour into muffin tins coated with cooking spray and bake 20 to 25 minutes. Serve warm or freeze.

*Makes 12 muffins*

# Breakfast Apple Pie

Apple pie is an American favorite, so why not have this no flour, no sugar version for breakfast?

1½ cups water
1 cup quick-cooking oats
1 apple, cored, peeled, and sliced
1 teaspoon Splenda
½ teaspoon ground cinnamon
⅔ cup nonfat milk

*"I've been following your No Flour, No Sugar Diet for about eighteen months. I've lost fifty pounds, and it's been easy, too. Thanks."*

*Dorothy, Anadarko, Oklahoma*

Mix water, oats, apple, Splenda, and cinnamon in microwave-safe bowl. Heat 2 minutes. Divide into 2 bowls. Pour milk over top of each bowl before serving.

*Serves 2*

# Fruity Granola

Full of flavor and crunch, this granola is great not only for breakfast but as a quick pick-me-up snack as well. One batch goes a long way and it keeps well.

1 cup dried whole dates, pitted
2 large bananas, chopped
2 tablespoons ground cinnamon
1 cup hot water
One 1-pound canister old-fashioned rolled oats
½ pound shredded unsweetened coconut
1 pound walnuts, chopped
1½ cups dried blueberries, cherries, cranberries, strawberries
    or any combination of dried fruits
2 cups golden raisins
Splenda to taste

Preheat oven to 250 degrees.

In blender, combine dates, bananas, cinnamon, and water. Mix until smooth. If mixture is too thick, add more hot water, 1 tablespoon at a time. In large bowl, mix together oats and banana mixture until coated. Break up any very large clusters. Stir in coconut. Spread thin layer on baking sheet. (This must be done in batches.) Bake, stirring occasionally, to desired crunchiness, about 1 hour.

Remove from oven and cool. Stir in walnuts, dried fruit, and raisins. Store in airtight containers. Sprinkle with Splenda before serving, if desired.

*Serves 20*

# Vegetarian Breakfast Casserole

This meatless breakfast will become one of your favorites.

6 ounces meatless sausage
6 eggs
¾ cup nonfat milk
¼ cup shredded cheddar cheese
¼ cup chopped green onion
Cooking spray, for coating
Salt and black pepper to taste
½ cup halved grape tomatoes

Preheat oven to 350 degrees.

Brown sausage according to package directions.

In large bowl, whisk eggs and milk. Add sausage, cheese, and onion. Pour into 8" x 8" baking dish coated with cooking spray. Bake 30 minutes, or until eggs are fully cooked. Remove from oven and cool slightly. Add salt and pepper. Slice into quarters. Serve topped with tomatoes.

*Serves 4*

# Eggs in Nests

These are fun, and tasty too. Make extra white rice at dinnertime, and you'll be all set to pop these in the oven the next morning.

Cooking spray, for coating
3 cups cooked rice
6 eggs
Salt and black pepper to taste
Paprika to taste
1 cup grated cheddar cheese

Preheat oven to 350 degrees.

Coat 6 cups of large muffin tin with cooking spray. Put ½ cup rice in each cup and press with spoon to form "nests." Break 1 egg into each, taking care not to break yolks. Sprinkle with salt, pepper, and paprika.

Bake about 25 minutes until eggs are set. Top with cheese and return to oven additional 5 minutes. Carefully remove nests from muffin cups.

*Serves 6*

# Scrapple

This is traditionally served with maple syrup, so if you've got artificially sweetened syrup (no sugar added), go ahead and try it that way, or top with Figgy Date Syrup.

¼ cup chopped lean ham
1½ cups chicken broth
1½ cups nonfat milk
¾ cup cornmeal
1 teaspoon salt
¼ teaspoon black pepper
½ teaspoon dried sage
½ teaspoon dried thyme
⅛ teaspoon cayenne pepper
Cooking spray, for coating

Combine all ingredients in medium saucepan. Bring to a boil, stirring constantly, and cook until mixture thickens and pulls away from sides of pan, 5 to 10 minutes. Coat 4" x 8" loaf pan with cooking spray. Place cooked cornmeal mixture in pan and let cool. Once it's cool, cover and refrigerate 4 hours or overnight.

To serve, unmold scrapple. Cut into 8 slices. Coat skillet with cooking spray and fry slices until golden brown.

*Serves 4*

## Eggs Florentine

This is a very elegant dish for a brunch.

One 10-ounce package frozen spinach, thawed and squeezed
   dry
½ teaspoon garlic powder
One 3-ounce package light cream cheese
4 eggs, poached
Salt and black pepper to taste
3 ounces Swiss cheese, grated

In medium-size bowl, mix spinach, garlic powder, and cream cheese until well blended. Mound ¼ of spinach mixture on a plate. Top with 1 hot poached egg and season with salt and pepper. Sprinkle with ¼ of the grated cheese. Heat in microwave for a few seconds to melt the cheese, if desired. Repeat for other servings. Serve.

*Serves 4*

## Green Eggs and Ham

This was inspired by a favorite Dr. Seuss book.

6 eggs
Green food coloring (optional)
½ cup frozen spinach, thawed and squeezed dry
Salt and black pepper to taste
4 ounces cooked ham, diced
Cooking spray, for coating

Break eggs into medium-size bowl and beat. Add a few drops of food coloring and mix until eggs are green. Season spinach with salt and pepper, then add to eggs. Mix in ham.

Coat skillet with cooking spray and place on stove over medium heat. When skillet is hot, add egg mixture. Stir eggs with spatula, cooking evenly. Cook about 4 or 5 minutes until eggs are set. Serve immediately.

*Serves 4*

# Salmon Omelet with Capers

This dish is very elegant as well as healthful, since salmon is full of omega-3 oils. This is a good way to use leftover salmon.

Cooking spray, for coating
4 eggs, beaten
½ cup cooked salmon, flaked
1 tablespoon capers, drained, plus more for garnish
Salt and black pepper to taste

Coat skillet generously with cooking spray and heat over medium heat. When skillet is hot, add eggs. Do not stir. Swirl eggs to fill bottom of skillet. Lift edges of egg mixture to allow uncooked egg to run to bottom of skillet. When egg is set but not completely cooked (about 2 minutes), sprinkle ½ of egg with salmon and capers. Fold other ½ over salmon and capers. Continue to cook 3 to 4 more minutes. Slide omelet onto plate and season with salt and pepper. Garnish with a few capers and serve.

*Serves 2*

# Baked Bacon and Egg Cups

This is an easy recipe to double or triple. It's good for a brunch party, too. You can prepare the bacon ahead of time, then assemble the dish just before your guests arrive. Pop it into the oven ten minutes before you're ready to eat.

4 strips bacon
Cooking spray, for coating
¼ cup sugar-free salsa
4 eggs
Salt and black pepper to taste
4 canned sugar-free pineapple rings, drained

Preheat oven to 350 degrees.

Cook bacon in skillet until nearly done but still flexible. Coat 4 cups of muffin tin with cooking spray. Line sides of muffin cups with bacon slices. Place 1 tablespoon salsa in bottom of each cup. Break 1 egg into each cup, taking care not to break yolk. Season with salt and pepper.

Bake about 10 minutes, or until eggs are set but not completely done. Remove eggs with spatula, set on pineapple rings, and serve.

*Serves 2*

# Potato Pancakes with Applesauce

A traditional Scandinavian dish, this is enjoyed in many parts of the United States. Serve with sliced fresh fruit.

2 medium red potatoes, grated, not peeled
2 tablespoons dried minced onion
1 egg, beaten

½ teaspoon salt
Black pepper to taste
Cooking spray, for coating
1 cup unsweetened applesauce

Mix potatoes, onion, egg, salt, and pepper. Coat pan with cooking spray and preheat over medium heat. With measuring cup, drop about ½ cup potato mixture into hot pan for each pancake. Cook about 4 minutes per side, or until golden brown.

Top each pancake with ¼ cup applesauce and serve.

*Serves 2*

# Crunchy Sunrise Parfait

Feel free to vary the types of berries and the flavor of yogurt. (This includes plain yogurt as well.) The different textures of smooth dairy and crunchy cereal make a very interesting breakfast.

2 cups frozen sugar-free raspberries, thawed
Splenda to taste
1 cup fat-free cottage cheese
1 cup sugar-free lemon yogurt
½ cup granola

Sweeten thawed raspberries with Splenda, if desired. In parfait or other tall glass, layer ¼ cup raspberries, ¼ cup cottage cheese, ¼ cup raspberries, ¼ cup yogurt, 2 tablespoons granola. Repeat in other 3 glasses and serve.

*Serves 4*

**10**

## *Snacks*

Americans love to snack, and not always on the right foods. It isn't easy passing up chips, candy bars, ice cream, cookies, and the host of other delectable—and fattening—morsels stocked in abundance on your local grocer's shelves.

While grocery shopping, have you noticed that the empty-calorie delights are at eye level to attract your immediate attention? The temptation to buy can be enormous when a bag of your favorite double-chocolate-coconut-caramel-marshmallow-swirl cookies stares you in the face. And this isn't by chance. Retailers know these items are often impulse purchases. Just look at the ubiquitous candy bar displays next to checkout counters. How often do you round a corner to the next aisle only to see an end shelf display of something tempting, tasty, and loaded with flour and sugar? Clever, isn't it?

Here are some strategies to use when it comes to snacks:

1. Make a snack grocery list. Sit down and give this some thought. Look through the recipes in this chapter for ideas. Include foods you will enjoy—certainly the fresh veggies and fruits I've spent so much time talking about, as well as other things such as sugar-free gelatins, 100 percent juice concentrate (for ice-cube Popsicles), dry-roasted almonds, popcorn, and flavored, unsweetened sparkling water. Put the

list on your refrigerator door so when you think of something else you can write it down.

Next, plan a trip to your grocery store at a time when you are not rushed or hungry. Check out the special or ethnic foods sections for snacks you might not know about—just being sure to read the labels and to avoid flour and sugar. Take a chance on foods you normally wouldn't try. You might be pleasantly surprised.

2. When you are at the store, try to avoid the snack food aisles. If you don't see it, you won't buy it. And if you don't take it home, you can't be tempted to eat it. Simple.

3. Keep your pantry well stocked with healthful snacks at all times. Consider dry-roasted nuts, flavored rice cakes, and unsweetened peanut butter for spreading on celery or toasted flourless bread.

4. Stock your refrigerator with the right foods. How often has each of us stood with the refrigerator door open, searching aimlessly for anything good to snack on? Having plenty of healthful snacks eliminates this and might even keep your electric bill down. Use zipper bags to store prepared servings of cut-up mushrooms, celery sticks, carrots, broccoli florets, pepper slices, and other raw vegetables. If you find munching on fresh vegetables alone too bland, keep a container of a fat-free, sugar-free dip on hand. Here's a recipe for a zesty dip made with a bean and yogurt base: in a blender, puree one 15-ounce can of black beans with ½ cup of sugar-free salsa until smooth. Spoon into a bowl and stir in ½ cup of fat-free plain yogurt, ¼ teaspoon of cumin, and 2 tablespoons of chopped fresh cilantro. Experiment with other no flour, no sugar ingredients and invent your own dips.

Have fat-free or low-fat cottage cheese and lean lunch meat in your refrigerator. Make a mini-wrap with the lunch meat by rolling it inside a lettuce leaf. Make up a few single-serving fruit parfaits by placing diced fresh fruit in several small bowls. Spoon no-fat, no-sugar-added vanilla yogurt on top of the fruit. Finish off the parfaits with a sprinkling of unsalted nuts.

5. Keep a bowl of apples, cherries, plums, grapes, pears, apricots,

or other washed fresh fruit on your kitchen counter where they are easy to reach.

6. Take your own snack to work. Some vending machines have started offering healthful snacks such as apples and fruit juices right alongside the candy and chips. This is a good thing. But why tempt yourself? Pack a snack.

Taking your own snack with you applies to places other than work as well. Headed out for a full morning of shopping? Instead of popping into the candy shop when your stomach starts growling, take along a bag of orange segments to eat while sitting on a sunny bench. Love to go to the movies? You didn't hear it from me, but there is no reason to stand in line to pay exorbitant prices for food you shouldn't be eating if an apple happens to be in your coat pocket.

7. Don't snack when you aren't hungry. Just because food is around, you don't have to munch on it. This leads to oversnacking, which just adds calories.

8. Have a snack between meals. It is thought that the practice of eating small portions throughout the day rather than one or two large meals is a healthier choice. One study revealed that the stomach capacity was actually reduced in people who regularly ate smaller, more frequent meals. People who do this are likely, over time, to feel more satisfied with less food. This might be why these people tend to be thinner.

9. Use this book. When you want a cookie, bake a batch of the Banana Oatmeal Cookies (see page 231). Prepare the snacks in this chapter ahead of time so you'll have them ready when you want them. These are much healthier choices and you will find them very satisfying.

10. Get your family on board. They are probably already programmed to reach for chips and store-bought cookies. Reprogramming yourself isn't an easy chore and it is likely to take a little more time to bring the others around to a more healthful way of addressing snack time. Just remind them it is for their own good.

Make every attempt to avoid the high-calorie, quick-fix snacks. Substitute better choices and you'll be pleased with the results.

# Fruit and Nut Bars

Snack bars are in everyone's diet as quick pick-me-ups. Try this recipe for delicious bars that are crunchy and filled with a combination of fruit and nuts.

¾ cup chopped dried dates
¾ cup chopped dried figs
½ cup water
½ cup coarsely chopped walnuts
½ cup coarsely chopped almonds
½ cup coarsely chopped cashews
1 cup raisins
¼ teaspoon vanilla extract
⅛ teaspoon ground cinnamon

Preheat oven to 350 degrees.

In blender, combine dates, figs, and water and blend until smooth. Place all ingredients in medium bowl and combine well. Press into 8" x 8" pan and bake 15 minutes. Cool and cut into squares before serving.

*Serves 12*

## Sweet Nut Snack

*Vi Evans, Lakeside, Oregon*

These sugar-free candied nuts make an excellent snack by themselves or add new flavor to chopped fruit, yogurt, and a green salad.

   4 tablespoons butter
   2 cups walnut halves
   ½ cup granular Splenda
   ⅛ cup vanilla extract
   3 tablespoons ground cinnamon
   ⅛ teaspoon ground nutmeg

In large nonstick skillet, melt butter over medium heat. When butter is bubbling, add nuts. Stir 3 minutes, coating nuts well. Sprinkle Splenda and vanilla over nuts and stir. Remove from heat. Add cinnamon and nutmeg. Stir well.

Remove from skillet and cool on paper plates or towels. Store in airtight container.

*Serves 8*

## Frozen Grapes

If you've never tried frozen grapes, you are in for a treat. This simple snack can be prepared in no time and is handy when a treat is in order. Frozen grapes have the versatility of being an appetizer, snack, or dessert. The "frosted" coating makes them an easy finger food.

   1 pound red seedless grapes
   Two 0.3-ounce packages sugar-free grape gelatin

Wash grapes and remove from stems. Place gelatin in shallow bowl and add individual grapes, 1 handful at a time. Completely coat grapes with gelatin. Transfer grapes to 1 or more freezer bags and store in freezer until ready to serve.

*Serves many*

# Fruit and Nut Trail Mix

*Annie Wilma Dalrymple, Pelzer, South Carolina*

This recipe can be modified when you substitute your favorite dried fruits or nuts. Have fun experimenting.

½ cup dried apricots, cut into quarters
½ cup halved dried dates
¼ cup raisins
½ cup whole almonds
½ cup walnut halves
½ cup unsalted peanuts
¼ cup unsalted sunflower seeds

Toss all ingredients together. Store in tightly covered container.

*Makes 3 cups*

# Tortillas, Portuguese Style

*Jackie Stewart, Killeen, Texas*

Are you looking for a crunchy, spicy snack? This might be just what the doctor ordered. It's full of taste, but feel free to add sugar-free salsa for a little extra zing.

12 corn tortillas (made with corn, not corn flour), cut into ¼"
   strips
1 to 2 tablespoons extra virgin olive oil
1 can Rotel green chiles
1 small onion, diced
2 cloves garlic, diced
½ cup grated cheddar cheese

Preheat oven to 350 degrees.

Fry tortilla strips in oil until crisp. Add chiles, onion, and garlic, mixing well. Pour into ovenproof baking dish and cover with cheese. Bake until heated and cheese melts. Serve.

*Serves 6 to 8*

# Sweet-and-Sour Nuts

This crunchy, sweet-and-sour snack is sure to satisfy. It's a great snack to accompany a movie.

4 tablespoons butter
1 cup pecan halves
½ cup cashews
½ cup almonds
3 tablespoons lemon extract
½ cup Splenda

Melt butter in frying pan over medium heat. Add nuts. Cook, stirring, about 4 minutes. Add lemon and Splenda, blending well, and continue cooking another 3 minutes. Remove from heat.

Transfer mixture to paper towels to cool. Store in individual snack bags.

*Serves 8*

## Cheesy Meat Crisps

What could be more simple than this snack? Take extra care when turning your meat slices so they don't break. If you do break some, sprinkle the pieces over a green salad in place of fatty bacon. They will taste slightly smoky with a crisp texture.

12 thin slices prosciutto
12 slices Swiss cheese

Preheat oven to 325 degrees.

Spread slices of prosciutto out on 2 baking sheets. Bake about 8 minutes, or until crisp, turning once. Place 1 cheese slice on each meat slice and return to oven until cheese is hot and bubbly, about 3 minutes. Remove from oven and cool slightly before serving.

*Serves 12*

*"Why do people still try all of the other ways to lose weight when your no flour, no sugar way is so simple? My husband lost fifty pounds on your diet and has kept it off. He is a man who has always had a sweet tooth, but we have found many things with no sugar added. People who haven't seen him for a few months cannot believe how much weight he has lost. I am so proud of him."*

*Pat, Stigler, Oklahoma*

# Chewy Granola Bars

You can modify this snack recipe to include your favorite dried fruits. You might enjoy varying the nuts each time you prepare it as well. This is a snack that can be taken to work and eaten as a mid-morning boost. It is sure to keep you going until lunchtime, or later.

2 cups quick-cooking oats
¼ cup chopped almonds
¼ cup chopped walnuts
¼ cup dried cranberries
¼ cup chopped dried dates
1 cup Figgy Date Syrup (see page 54)
2 tablespoons extra virgin olive oil
Cooking spray, for coating

Preheat oven to 350 degrees.

Combine all ingredients in medium bowl. Coat 6" x 6" baking dish with cooking spray. Transfer mixture to baking dish and pat down to about ¼" thick. Bake 20 to 25 minutes. Slice into 6 bars when cool.

If there are any left over, wrap them in waxed paper to keep them moist.

*Serves 6*

# Layered Melon Ice Pops

This kid-friendly summer treat is sure to please everyone. You'll love the nutritious results and you'll be pleased with the colors and tastes.

½ watermelon
1 cantaloupe

4 kiwifruits, peeled
Popsicle sticks

Remove seeds from melons and cut fruit into pieces. Blend each fruit separately in blender. In ice pop holders or medium paper cups, fill ⅓ full with watermelon. Allow to freeze. Layer next ⅓ with kiwifruit. When kiwifruit is about half frozen, place in Popsicle sticks and allow to finish freezing. Top off with cantaloupe. Ready to eat when fully frozen.

*Serves many*

# Leftover Baked Potato Skins

When you next plan mashed potatoes for a meal, bake the potatoes first. Slice them lengthwise and scoop the pulp from the skins. Transfer the potato to a bowl or pan and mash and prepare as you ordinarily would. Save the skins for this snack.

6 medium scooped-out potato skins (12 halves)
1 tablespoon olive oil
½ teaspoon garlic powder
Black pepper to taste

Preheat oven to 350 degrees.
Slice potato skins in half lengthwise, making 24 pieces. In small bowl, combine olive oil with garlic powder and pepper. Drizzle over potato skins. Bake 10 minutes, or until golden brown. Serve warm.

*Serves 8 to 12*

# Orange Smoothie

This drink will hit the spot if you are looking for a cold refreshing change.

1 all-fruit sugar-free frozen orange juice bar
8 ounces orange juice
4 ounces plain yogurt
6 ice cubes, crushed

Remove and discard stick from bar. Place all ingredients in blender and mix until smooth. Pour into 2 glasses and add straws. Drink immediately.

*Serves 2*

# Yum-yum Balls

*Lavina Weaver, Newmanstown, Pennsylvania*

This is a good snack when you're on the go. Take a few to work with you in a zipper bag for a quick, tasty treat during the day.

4 ounces low-fat cream cheese, softened
¼ cup toasted sunflower seeds
4 tablespoons sugar-free crunchy peanut butter
¼ cup oat bran
¼ cup wheat germ
2 tablespoons chopped nuts
½ cup sugar-free shredded coconut

Mix all ingredients except coconut in bowl. Shape into small balls. Coat with coconut. Refrigerate until ready to serve.

*Serves 8*

# Apricot Orange Balls

Use good-quality, soft apricots for this snack. Take the liberty of replacing the walnuts with shredded coconut for a different taste.

1 pound dried apricots, chopped
1 seedless orange, peeled and chopped
½ cup finely ground walnuts
1 individual packet Splenda

Mix apricots and orange in food processor until doughy texture forms. Remove from food processor and shape into 20 small balls. Blend ground walnuts and Splenda. Place walnut mixture in shallow bowl or plate and roll fruit balls until well coated. Store in tightly covered container until ready to serve.

*Makes 20 fruit balls*

# Tostadas

*Maureen Shirley, Simi Valley, California*

What could be more satisfying than a crunchy tostada as a quick snack?

4 corn tortillas
1 cup low-fat refried beans
¾ cup shredded cheddar cheese
1 cup shredded lettuce
½ cup shredded carrots
½ cup diced fresh tomato

Preheat oven to 350 degrees.

Bake tortillas on cookie sheet 10 minutes until crisp. Remove from oven. Top each tortilla with ¼ cup refried beans and ¼ of cheese. Return to oven and bake 2 to 3 minutes longer until beans are warm and cheese melts. Remove from oven, top with lettuce, carrots, and tomatoes divided evenly among tostadas, and serve.

*Serves 4*

# Peanut Butter Surprise Bites

These delightful bites are great to have as an after-school snack or as a midmorning pick-me-up.

1 cup chopped pecans
¼ cup raisins
1 tablespoon oat bran
One 16-ounce jar sugar-free peanut butter
1 tablespoon sugar-free apple juice
½ teaspoon ground cinnamon
1 individual packet Splenda

Place pecans, raisins, oat bran, peanut butter, and apple juice in bowl. Stir until well blended. Form into 24 small balls. On plate, blend cinnamon and Splenda. Roll balls in cinnamon mixture to coat completely. Store in closed container in refrigerator until ready to serve.

*Makes 24 balls*

# Homemade Tortilla Chips

While you can eat tortilla chips as long as you check the ingredients (make sure they don't have corn flour or sugar), these tortillas are better because they're baked, not fried, and you control the level of salt.

12 corn tortillas (made with corn, not corn flour)
Cooking spray, for coating
Salt to taste (optional)

Preheat oven to 425 degrees.

With scissors or sharp knife, cut each tortilla into 6 wedges. Place tortilla wedges on baking sheet coated with cooking spray. If you wish to use salt, lightly spray tortillas with cooking spray, then lightly sprinkle with salt. Turn over and repeat.

Bake 5 to 8 minutes, or until tortillas begin to turn golden brown and crispy. Watch closely and do not let them burn.

*Makes 6 servings*

# Pico de Gallo (Fresh Salsa)

Use fully ripened fresh tomatoes for this. If they are unavailable, use drained canned tomatoes instead. If fresh cilantro is unavailable, skip it altogether. The dried version doesn't add the zing.

2 medium tomatoes, seeded and chopped, or 2 cups
    well-drained canned tomatoes
½ medium red onion, minced
1 green bell pepper, chopped
1 or 2 jalapeños, seeded and chopped, to taste
¼ cup chopped fresh cilantro
½ teaspoon salt, or to taste
1 tablespoon lime juice (optional)

Combine all ingredients in small bowl. Serve with Homemade Tortilla Chips (page 79).

*Serves 6*

# Banana Oat Cookies

Yes, a healthier version of cookies! And yes, there's oil in them, so don't go crazy. You can enjoy a cookie or two once in a while on this diet and the kids will love them.

3 large bananas
¾ cup chopped walnuts
¼ cup canola or vegetable oil
1 teaspoon vanilla extract
2 cups quick-rolled oats
¾ cup dried blueberries
⅛ teaspoon ground cinnamon
½ teaspoon salt

Preheat oven to 350 degrees.

Mash bananas with potato masher or fork. Mix in nuts, oil, and vanilla. Stir in oats, blueberries, cinnamon, and salt. Let sit about 10 minutes. Drop by rounded teaspoons onto lightly greased cookie sheet.

Bake 18 to 23 minutes until golden brown. Watch closely to keep them from burning. Let cool completely before serving or storing in airtight container.

*Makes 30 cookies*

# Black and Blue Nachos

Make sure your tortilla chips are made with corn, not corn flour. Or make your own (see my recipe for Homemade Tortilla Chips, page 79), so you can control the fat and salt.

4 ounces blue corn tortilla chips
1 cup canned black beans, drained, rinsed, and patted dry
1 cup shredded cheddar cheese
½ cup shredded Monterey Jack cheese
¼ cup black olives, sliced
Pickled jalapeño rings to taste

Place tortilla chips on large microwave-safe dinner plate or medium-size platter. Spoon beans and both cheeses over top. Sprinkle with olives and jalapeño rings.

Put plate in microwave and heat 2 to 5 minutes, or until cheese is melted. Serve immediately.

*Serves 4*

# Herbed Popcorn

Air-popped popcorn makes a good snack, but it doesn't always have a lot of flavor. This is a way to add flavor without a lot of fat.

¼ cup popcorn (5 cups popped)
¼ teaspoon garlic powder
½ teaspoon dried basil
½ teaspoon dried parsley
1 tablespoon grated Parmesan cheese
Butter-flavored cooking spray

Pop popcorn in hot-air popper or in microwave popper without oil. In small dish, mix together garlic, basil, parsley, and cheese. Place popcorn in large bowl and spray with butter-flavored cooking spray, stirring to coat. Sprinkle herb mixture over and toss to coat.

*Serves 2*

# Exotic Peanuts

When you season your own peanuts, you've got complete control. No added fat, no unpronounceable ingredients. You can add a bit of salt to these if you like, but the spices add enough zip so that you don't need it. These are great for a party.

1 teaspoon curry powder
½ teaspoon cayenne pepper
¼ teaspoon garlic powder
Cooking spray, for coating
3 cups raw, unsalted peanuts

Preheat oven to 300 degrees.

In small dish, combine curry, cayenne, and garlic.

Coat baking sheet with cooking spray. Spread peanuts on sheet and then lightly cover with additional cooking spray. Sprinkle spice mixture over peanuts and toss to coat evenly. Bake 15 minutes, stirring occasionally, or until peanuts are lightly toasted. Serve.

*Serves 6*

# Sweet Cheesy Celery

Many Americans grew up with stuffed celery as a snack. This adds some interest with apricots and almonds.

8 or more celery stalks, cleaned and trimmed
4 ounces low-fat cream cheese
2 tablespoons nonfat milk
1 tablespoon finely chopped dried apricots
1 tablespoon finely chopped almonds

Cut celery stalks into 3" segments (you should have 32 pieces). In small bowl, mix together cream cheese, milk, apricots, and almonds. With spoon, fill each piece of celery with cheese mixture. Serve immediately or cover and chill until ready to eat.

*Serves 8*

## Creamy Peanut Dip with Apples

This is a healthful snack, full of vitamins and protein. If this is going to sit for more than a minute or two before serving, toss the apple slices with a teaspoon or so of lemon juice to keep them from browning.

¼ cup smooth sugar-free natural peanut butter
2 tablespoons orange juice
1 tablespoon lemon juice
½ cup nonfat plain yogurt
⅛ teaspoon vanilla extract
2 medium apples, cored and sliced in eighths

In small bowl, combine peanut butter and orange and lemon juices. Mix until smooth. Stir in yogurt and vanilla. Serve immediately with sliced apples.

*Serves 2*

## Black Bean Dip

Beans are full of nutrients and high in fiber. This is a quick, low-fat version of a bean dip. You can also make this with canned pinto beans instead of black beans.

One 15-ounce can black beans, drained and rinsed
One 4-ounce can mild green chiles, chopped
1 tablespoon cider vinegar
1½ teaspoons chili powder
¼ teaspoon garlic powder
¼ teaspoon onion powder

Place all ingredients in blender or food processor and blend until smooth. Transfer to bowl to serve.

*Serves 8*

# Vegetable "Nachos"

A healthier version of a Southwestern favorite. Jicama is an exotic Southwestern vegetable that looks unattractive, but once you peel away the outer skin, you'll find that it tastes crisp and crunchy, rather like a savory apple.

1 cup jicama, peeled and cut into finger-size sticks
1 medium red bell pepper, sliced into strips
1 large zucchini, sliced
3 or 4 celery stalks, cut into 4" sticks
1½ cups shredded Pepper Jack cheese
2 tablespoons diced, mild, canned green chiles
2 tablespoons sliced black olives

Arrange vegetables on large microwave-safe dinner plate or small platter. Sprinkle evenly with cheese, chiles, and olives. Microwave 2 to 5 minutes on medium high until cheese melts. Serve.

*Serves 12*

# Plantain Chips

Plantains may look like large green bananas, but they are a starchy tropical fruit that is typically fried, sautéed, or baked. You can even put them in soups or stews, as you would a sweet potato.

2 large green plantains
Salt to taste
Cooking spray, for coating

Peel plantains, then slice as thinly as possible. Place slices in large bowl of salted water and soak about 30 minutes. Drain and pat dry with paper towels.

Coat skillet with cooking spray. Place in as many plantains as will comfortably fit without crowding. Cook over medium heat 3 to 4 minutes, turning once, until golden brown. Remove to drain on paper towels. Cook in batches until all plantains have been cooked, using more cooking spray as necessary. Serve.

*Serves 2*

> *"I have never been overweight but always had an extra ten pounds that bothered me. Even with exercise and limiting calories, I could never keep them off permanently. It's only been ten days, but I have effortlessly lost three pounds and the weight is steadily going down. An unexpected side effect is that I wake up very easily in the morning and no longer have a groggy feeling. I've started working out regularly and actually have energy to do it! I intend to make this my lifelong commitment."*
>
> *Janna, Tallahassee, Florida*

# *Appetizers*

We tend to think of appetizers as fancy, expensive, loaded with unwanted calories, and an unnecessary part of a meal. And frankly, appetizers are often all of these things. But they don't have to be. There are many simple, nutritious, inexpensive choices when it comes to appetizers. Healthful appetizers can actually cause you to eat smaller entrée portions and thus fewer calories overall in the meal.

Of course, in today's chaotic world, to prepare appetizers seven days a week might be a bit much. But if you decide to turn a mundane Thursday evening into a special time, or you are entertaining guests, appetizers might be just what the doctor ordered.

## Relish This

Years ago many eateries routinely served a relish plate as a complimentary appetizer. It was a good idea then and it is now. Below is a list of quick and simple ingredients to mix and match for your own relish plate. Have fun with this. Begin with a plate covered with fresh, crisp lettuce leaves, then arrange each item like a spoke in a wheel. Alternate colors to make the presentation more attractive.

- Broccoli and cauliflower florets
- Green, red, orange, and yellow bell pepper wedges

- Cherry tomatoes
- Fresh raw mushrooms
- Zucchini spears
- Cucumber slices
- Carrot sticks—"Baby carrots" are available bagged and ready to eat. Not only do these work as appetizers, but you can take the bag with the leftovers to work with you for a midmorning snack.
- Celery sticks—These can be served plain or filled with low-fat cream cheese.
- Olives—Today there are often "olive bars" in most supermarkets where you can select from many delicious types. For variety, look for stuffed green olives.
- Salted edamame—These soybeans in the pod have gained popularity here in the United States, along with Japanese restaurants that feature them.
- Avocado slices—Squeeze fresh lime juice over these for a bit more zest.
- Pickles
- Marinated artichoke hearts
- Dry-roasted almonds or other nuts—If you are watching your sodium intake, unsalted varieties are available.
- Pepperoncini and other pickled peppers
- Cold cooked shrimp
- Grilled chicken breast diced into bite-size pieces—Serve cold or hot.
- Cubes of low-fat or nonfat cheeses—Low-fat cheeses were once a poor-tasting substitute for the whole milk versions, but this has since changed and there are a number of good low-fat cheeses on the market today. Naturally, on my No Flour, No Sugar Diet, regular cheese is allowed, but give these cheeses a try. They can only benefit your health and cholesterol levels.

When you serve your relish dish, provide small plates, cocktail napkins, and toothpicks. Supply nonfat, low-fat, or no-sugar-added sauces for dipping if you like.

## Salsa

Salsa is another great choice for an appetizer. This healthful tomato concoction is available in most supermarket delicatessen sections, or, if you have the time, make it yourself. Serve it on the side to spoon over fresh veggies. Or serve it with baked whole corn tortilla chips. You can prepare your own chips by cutting corn tortillas into wedge-shaped pieces, spraying the wedges with olive oil, and baking them at 350 degrees, turning them once, until crisp.

## Fruit

Consider fresh fruit. Rather than simply cutting fruit up and placing it in a bowl, thread pieces of fruit on bamboo skewers. Apple and pineapple chunks with red seedless grapes make a good combination. Serve on top of lettuce leaves with a dollop of plain yogurt on the side. It's simple, quick, and nutritious, and the fancy presentation will make it all the more enticing.

## Shrimp

Want something a tad more elegant? Consider a shrimp cocktail. You can make your own cocktail sauce by combining 1 cup sugar-free ketchup, 2 tablespoons lemon juice, and ¼ teaspoon hot pepper sauce. If you prefer, eliminate the hot pepper sauce and add prepared horseradish, using as much as your taste buds deem appropriate.

If time is a consideration, you can purchase cocktail sauce already made; just check the label to be sure there isn't any added sugar. Your shrimp can be cooked at home, then chilled, or purchased ready to eat.

To serve, place lettuce or spinach leaves on individual plates and add a generous dollop of the sauce to the center. Surround the sauce with four or five shrimp in a pinwheel effect, with the tails toward the outside of the plate. Serve a wedge of fresh lemon on each plate to be drizzled over the shrimp. While you might want to add more shrimp, consider that this is only an appetizer—a prelude of what's to follow.

## Oysters

Are you still wishing for something elegant but prefer to spend even less time in the kitchen? Fresh oysters on the half shell are a good choice. Asking your local fish market to open the shells for you makes your job easier. Serve four to each person on a bed of crushed ice. Supply lemon wedges and Tabasco sauce for those who want them. Total calories—50! Nice.

## Baked Brie

Another attractive and very simple appetizer is Brie cheese. Warm a round of Brie in a 325-degree oven ten to fifteen minutes. Serve with apple and pear wedges with the skins left on and small knives for slicing the warm cheese onto the fruit.

While the Brie is a delight by itself, you might consider adding a light fruit glaze over the top. Use apricot Simply Fruit, which can be found in the jam and jelly section of most grocery stores. A thin covering spread over the cheese before it is placed in the oven will make a statement when placed in the center of your table for your family and guests to enjoy.

The recipes in this chapter give you even more choices for nutrient-rich no-flour, no-sugar appetizers. Whatever you choose, pay a bit of extra attention to making this first course attractive and satisfying.

# Triple-Cheese Crabmeat-Stuffed Mushrooms

*Melanie Spillman, Memphis, Tennessee*

This recipe is very low in carbohydrates, simple, and easy to prepare. Your friends and family will gobble them up.

Two 8-ounce packages baby portobello mushrooms
Drizzle of extra virgin olive oil
1 pound lump crabmeat, shredded, shell pieces removed
½ cup shredded mozzarella cheese
½ cup shredded Parmesan cheese
½ cup crumbled feta cheese

Preheat oven to 350 degrees.

Remove stems from mushrooms. Wipe clean with damp paper towel. Place mushroom caps upside down in baking dish. Drizzle lightly with oil. Fill each mushroom cap with crabmeat. Layer with mozzarella, Parmesan, and feta, in that order.

Bake 15 to 25 minutes, depending on size of mushrooms. Mushrooms should be fork tender and cheese should be melted and bubbly. Serve immediately.

*Serves 8 to 12*

## Cranberry and Cherry Jell-O on Spinach

*Noreen Walker, Columbiaville, Michigan*

While this versatile dish may sound like a dessert, it makes an excellent appetizer or brunch plate with its unique flavor and red-and-green color scheme. For an added bonus, place cooked brown rice on top of the spinach leaves with the cranberry gelatin on top of that. Fresh or frozen cranberries can be used.

> One 12-ounce bag cranberries
> 3 cups water
> 1 cup Splenda
> One 0.6-ounce (large) package sugar-free cherry Jell-O
> ½ cup chopped walnuts
> One 20-ounce can sugar-free crushed pineapple, with juice
> Fresh spinach leaves, rinsed well and dried

Rinse cranberries and place in saucepan. Add 1 cup cold water and Splenda. Bring to a boil, stirring occasionally, and simmer about 10 minutes, or until berries pop and thicken. Set aside.

Put Jell-O in medium bowl. Add 2 cups boiling water. Stir 3 minutes. Add cooked cranberries, walnuts, and pineapple. Mix well and pour into 8" x 8" dish. Refrigerate 4 to 6 hours, or until set. To serve, place spinach leaves on each plate and top with 2" x 4" rectangles of gelatin.

*Serves 8*

## Mozzarella with Tomato and Basil

The color combination of this presentation is always striking. Infuse your oil with the basil leaves and seasonings for a crisp, distinctive flavor.

12 fresh basil leaves, julienned
¼ cup extra virgin olive oil
Salt and black pepper to taste
1 pound fresh mozzarella, cut into 12 slices
2 large vine-ripened tomatoes, cut into 12 slices

Place basil in shallow dish with oil, salt, and pepper and let stand for ½ hour. Place 3 slices of cheese on each of 4 dessert plates. Cover each with 3 tomato slices. Drizzle basil and oil over top and serve.

*Serves 4*

# Crab-Filled Endive

Endive is a delicate French vegetable, with leaves in the shape of romaine lettuce. Its mild flavor is distinct, yet it is very light and its flavor makes for easy pairing with other items.

2 cans crabmeat
1 small red onion, finely chopped
1 green onion, finely chopped
1 clove garlic, finely chopped
1 tablespoon sugar-free mayonnaise
1 tablespoon nonfat plain yogurt
Salt and black pepper to taste
8 endive leaves, rinsed and dried

In medium bowl, mix together crabmeat, red and green onions, garlic, mayonnaise, and yogurt. Add salt and pepper to taste. Place endive on platter in pinwheel pattern. Divide crab mixture into leaves and serve.

*Serves 8*

# Stuffed Artichokes

This dish makes a beautiful presentation. It is sure to impress any guest.

> *"I just love the No Flour, No Sugar Diet. I'm a cancer survivor of two years and my doctor is so pleased with my twenty-five-pound weight loss and the fact that I'm feeling so good."*
>
> *Bonnie, Hanford, California*

6 medium-size artichokes, hearts reserved
12 baby asparagus spears, chopped
½ cup julienned carrot
¼ cup nonfat plain yogurt
¼ cup low-fat cream cheese
1 large can tuna in water, drained
Salt and black pepper to taste

Rinse artichokes in cold water, spreading leaves to ensure no grit remains. Pull off any small or discolored leaves at base. Cut off stem. Remove top ¼ of artichokes and tips of leaves, if desired. Place in large pot on steamer above 2" boiling water. Cover and steam about 30 minutes, or until center leaf pulls out easily. Add additional water during steaming if necessary. Carefully remove cone, any purple-tipped leaves, and fuzz from center of artichoke. Remove hearts, chop, and set aside.

In separate pot, blanch asparagus and carrot in salted boiling water 1 to 2 minutes. Cool. In medium bowl, combine yogurt, cream cheese, tuna, artichoke hearts, asparagus, carrot, salt, and pepper. Mix well.

Carefully scoop mixture into center of each artichoke. Place on individual dessert plates. Serve at room temperature.

*Serves 6*

# Tomatoes and Cottage Cheese

This simple dish makes an attractive presentation with its vibrant colors. And, it is a great start to your dinner.

4 plum tomatoes
2 cups frisée, rinsed and dried
Spritz of sugar-free raspberry vinegar dressing
½ cup low-fat cottage cheese
1 tablespoon chopped fresh chives, for garnish

Remove tops of tomatoes. Place tomatoes upright and cut each one into 4 wedges, being careful not to slice completely down. Place frisée on 4 dessert plates with 1 tomato in center of each, opening and fanning wedges downward toward plate. Each tomato should resemble a flower, with four "petals." Lightly spritz dressing over open tomato. Fill each center with ¼ cottage cheese. Garnish with chives.

*Serves 4*

## Cucumber Delights

Cucumbers resembling flower petals topped with crab make a delightful appetizer. They're easy to prepare and taste great.

1 English cucumber, skin left on and washed
1 small can crabmeat
2 teaspoons sugar-free mayonnaise
2 teaspoons nonfat plain yogurt
1 small red onion, diced
4 small fresh dill sprigs
4 lettuce leaves, rinsed and dried

With fork, pierce skin of cucumber along the length all around cucumber. This produces a flower-petal-like appearance when sliced. Cut cucumber into ½" slices, discarding both ends. Blend crabmeat, mayonnaise, yogurt, and onion in small bowl. Place spoonful of crab mixture on each cucumber slice and sprig of dill on top. To serve, place lettuce leaf and 3 cucumber slices on each of 4 small plates.

*Serves 4*

## Tomatoes Stuffed with Salmon

Picture a ripe red tomato filled with salmon, sitting on a bed of lettuce leaves. Talk about an appealing appetizer!

4 medium ripe tomatoes, rinsed and dried
1 cup canned salmon, flaked and deboned
2 teaspoons sugar-free mayonnaise
2 teaspoons nonfat plain yogurt
1 medium apple, cored, peeled, and cubed
Black pepper to taste

4 lettuce leaves, rinsed and dried
1 tablespoon chopped fresh chives, for garnish

Slice off tomato tops and scoop out centers, being careful not to pierce skins. Blend salmon, mayonnaise, yogurt, apple, and pepper in small bowl. To serve, place lettuce leaves on 4 dessert plates. Top with tomato shells placed upright. Fill each with ¼ of salmon mixture. Garnish with chives.

*Serves 4*

# Salmon Cakes on Spinach

Salmon cakes smell good and taste delicious. The patties can be prepared in advance and refrigerated until you are ready to heat them.

8 ounces salmon, cooked and flaked
1 egg, beaten
¼ cup instant mashed potato flakes
⅛ teaspoon paprika
⅛ teaspoon black pepper
½ teaspoon chopped fresh chives
Cooking spray, for coating
Spinach leaves, rinsed and dried

Combine all ingredients except spinach in small bowl. Form into 4 patties. Preheat frying pan coated with cooking spray over medium-high heat. Sauté salmon patties, turning once, until golden brown, about 8 minutes. Serve over spinach leaves on individual dessert plates.

*Serves 4*

# Shrimp Cocktail

Why not consider a traditional, tried-and-true appetizer that everyone seems to love? Buy the shrimp already cooked from your fish market. This will save you time that can be devoted to the preparation of your own sauce.

    1 cup diced plum tomatoes
    1 tablespoon sugar-free horseradish
    1 small clove garlic, minced
    1 teaspoon red wine vinegar
    1 teaspoon dry mustard
    Dash of pepper
    4 lettuce leaves, rinsed and dried
    16 large shrimp, cleaned and cooked
    1 small lemon, quartered, for garnish

In small bowl, mix together tomatoes, horseradish, garlic, vinegar, mustard, and pepper. Line 4 dessert plates with lettuce leaves. Place 4 shrimp on each plate, in pinwheel pattern. Scoop ¼ of cocktail sauce into each center. Serve chilled with lemon wedges.

*Serves 4*

# Potato Rosettes

You can make these appetizers look really elegant if you have a pastry bag (available at kitchen stores). Scoop the potato mixture into the bag and, using a decorative tip, squeeze rosette-shaped dollops onto a baking sheet.

2 cups mashed potatoes
1 egg, beaten
¼ cup shredded cheddar cheese
¼ teaspoon garlic powder
½ teaspoon salt (optional)
⅛ teaspoon black pepper
1 tablespoon chopped fresh chives
Cooking spray, for coating

Preheat broiler.

In large bowl, mix potato, egg, cheese, garlic powder, salt, pepper, and chives. Stir until well blended. Drop spoonfuls onto baking sheet coated with cooking spray, swirling spoon to give rosette look to potatoes. Broil 5 to 8 minutes, or until lightly browned and cheese is melted. Serve.

*Makes 2 dozen*

# Cheesy Eggplant Wedges

Because this dish is so rich and cheesy, be sure to serve it with a lean meat dish such as grilled chicken breasts sprinkled with a seasoned salt. The recipe calls for Japanese eggplants, which are smaller and tenderer than the usual variety.

8 Japanese eggplants or 1 regular eggplant
Cooking spray, for coating
1 teaspoon onion powder
1 teaspoon garlic powder
1½ cups grated cheddar cheese

Preheat broiler.

Peel and quarter eggplants lengthwise (if using regular eggplant, cut into smaller wedges). Place wedges on baking sheet and coat with cooking spray. Sprinkle ½ of onion and garlic powders on wedges. Broil 5 to 8 minutes until beginning to brown. Turn over and spray again with cooking spray and sprinkle on remaining onion and garlic powders. Broil 4 or 5 minutes longer. Cover with cheese. Broil again just long enough to melt cheese. Serve hot.

*Serves 4*

# Mini Quiches

You can vary these quiches by substituting different meats, vegetables, and cheeses.

¾ cup finely diced lean ham
¼ cup canned mild green chiles, drained and diced
2 tablespoons chopped fresh chives
1½ cups shredded jalapeño Jack cheese
2 eggs, beaten
¾ cup nonfat sour cream
Cooking spray, for coating

Preheat oven to 375 degrees.

In small bowl, mix ham, chiles, chives, and cheese. In another bowl, beat together eggs and sour cream.

Coat cups of a mini-muffin tin with cooking spray. Scoop 1 heaping teaspoon ham mixture into each cup, then add 1 teaspoon egg mixture. Bake until quiches are brown and puffy, 20 to 25 minutes. Cool in tin 5 minutes, then remove muffins and serve warm.

Variations: you can substitute a 6-ounce can of crabmeat for the ham, roasted red pepper for the green chiles, and Swiss cheese for the jalapeño Jack. Or you can make these with diced chicken breast, well-drained chopped spinach, and cheddar cheese.

*Makes 2 to 3 dozen*

# Sausage-Stuffed Mushrooms

A traditional party favorite, updated here to remove the bread crumbs. The turkey also provides a lower-fat alternative to the usual version.

20 large fresh button mushrooms
Cooking spray, for coating
2 tablespoons dry sherry
¼ pound Italian turkey sausage
¼ cup cooked rice
4 tablespoons grated Parmesan cheese

Preheat oven to 350 degrees.

Remove mushroom stems and finely chop them. Set aside.

Coat skillet with cooking spray. Sauté mushroom caps on medium-high heat 1 to 2 minutes. Add 1 tablespoon sherry and cook until evaporated, 1 to 2 minutes. Drain on paper towels.

Wipe out skillet. Cook sausage over medium-high heat until crumbled and browned, about 5 minutes. Add chopped mushroom stems and cook 2 minutes more. Remove from heat and drain.

In medium bowl, mix together sausage mixture, rice, 2 tablespoons cheese, and remaining sherry. Mound 1 rounded tablespoon onto each cap. Arrange stuffed caps on baking dish and bake 10 to 15 minutes. Sprinkle with remaining cheese. Serve warm.

*Makes 20*

# Ham and Date Roll-ups

Dates are very sweet, and the combination of sweet and salty will help calm your hunger.

20 pitted dried whole dates
Twenty 2" x 4" strips lean sliced ham
Cooking spray, for coating

Preheat oven to 350 degrees.

Place 1 date on 1 strip of ham. Roll and secure with toothpick. Repeat with remaining dates and ham. Place on baking sheet lightly coated with cooking spray and bake 9 to 12 minutes, or until heated through. Serve warm.

*Makes 20*

# Stuffed Celery

The combination of smooth cream cheese and a crunchy vegetable helps satisfy a lot of cravings. Use low-fat or nonfat cream cheese to reduce calories.

One 8-ounce package cream cheese, softened
½ cup canned sugar-free crushed pineapple, drained
½ teaspoon lemon juice
Dash of hot pepper sauce
6 or 8 celery stalks, cut into 3" pieces

Mix cream cheese, pineapple, lemon juice, and hot pepper sauce together in small bowl until well blended. Spoon about 1 tablespoon into each celery piece. Serve.

*Serves 6 to 8*

# Cowboy Caviar

This is a black-eyed pea salsa, but it seems there are almost as many variations of this as there are stars visible in a prairie sky. It can be modified with avocado, corn, and tomatoes. Some recipes use black beans instead of the black-eyed peas. However you make it, it's tasty and nutritious.

One 15-ounce can black-eyed peas, drained and rinsed
1 green bell pepper, diced
1 red bell pepper, diced
1 jalapeño chile, diced
1 red onion, diced
1 clove garlic, minced
2 tablespoons red wine vinegar
1½ teaspoons hot pepper sauce
1 teaspoon extra virgin olive oil
¼ cup chopped fresh cilantro
Tortilla chips (optional)

In large bowl, mix all ingredients. Let stand at least 1 hour at room temperature for flavors to blend. Serve with tortilla chips (homemade or store-bought with no sugar and corn flour), if desired.

*Serves 15*

# Hot Artichoke Dip

This is a party favorite, commonly found at most potluck gatherings. Making it yourself gives you control over the ingredients.

One 16-ounce can artichoke hearts, drained
½ cup low-fat cream cheese, softened
½ cup nonfat plain yogurt
½ cup frozen chopped spinach, squeezed dry
½ cup grated Parmesan cheese
1 teaspoon garlic powder
Salt and black pepper to taste
Tortilla chips (optional)
Celery sticks (optional)
Carrot sticks (optional)

Preheat oven to 350 degrees.

Chop artichoke hearts. In large bowl, blend artichoke hearts, cream cheese, yogurt, spinach, cheese, garlic, salt, and pepper until well mixed. Spoon into oven-safe dish and bake 25 to 30 minutes until hot. Serve with tortilla chips or celery and carrot sticks, if desired.

*Serves 12*

# Smoked Salmon Ball

Your guests will think you spent a lot of money buying this dish from a gourmet foods store. Use low-fat or nonfat cream cheese for reduced calories.

Two 7-ounce cans smoked salmon, flaked
One 8-ounce package low-fat cream cheese, softened
1 teaspoon prepared horseradish (no added sugar)
2 teaspoons lemon juice
1 tablespoon finely chopped red onion
¼ cup chopped fresh parsley
Carrot sticks (optional)
Celery sticks (optional)

Mix salmon, cream cheese, horseradish, lemon juice, and onion in medium bowl until well blended. Cover and refrigerate ½ hour or more. Form into ball and roll in parsley. Serve with carrot and celery sticks, if desired.

*Serves 10 to 12*

# Soups

Soups have been a mainstay at mealtime for many years. A first-century Roman named Marcus Gavius Apicius included a few soup recipes in his cookbook *De re coquinaria* two thousand years ago. Some cultures, such as the French, serve soup as often as three times a week. The Italians have long made a garlic bread soup that is both easy and delectable. Some claim it keeps vampires away and cures baldness, but, as a medical professional, I can't subscribe to either of these benefits.

To make Italian garlic bread soup, sauté 5 or 6 large fresh cloves garlic in a medium saucepan with enough olive oil to cover the bottom of the pan. Add ½ loaf of flourless, broken-up, stale bread—the drier the better—and toss with the oil and garlic. Slowly add about 2 cups of a broth of your choice. Heat. Stir lightly so the bread retains most of its shape.

## Not Just an Appetizer

Thought of first in the role of an appetizer in the United States, soups, especially the heartier ones, work very well as the main dish in a meal. They make great warming lunches on blustery winter days. The Italian Vegetable Soup, sent in by one of my readers, would satisfy the hungriest crowd if combined with a fresh salad. Some, such as my Dilled Cucumber Yogurt Soup, are served cold. This soup blends the snappy flavor of dill with the coolness of cucumbers and yogurt. Radish slices as a garnish add a touch of color and crunch.

## Soup Made with Leftovers

Make your own soup from leftovers. It will be simple and healthful and you are bound to have some leftovers that will work to make an excellent dish. In fact, many savvy and frugal cooks freeze small bags of leftovers in anticipation of combining them the next time they pull out their stockpots.

If you like, sauté some onions or garlic in a little olive oil in the bottom of a pan. Add canned stock, broth made from bouillon cubes, or stock you've made yourself. Then add a soup bone or whatever is left over from last Sunday's dinner. Cut meat into bite-size pieces and remove small bones. Consider including chopped fresh carrots or celery, cooked brown rice, frozen corn, canned beans, and canned tomatoes. In a real pinch, add mixed frozen vegetables from your freezer.

Heat the broth and added ingredients to just short of boiling, then lower the temperature, simmering until the vegetables soften, about fifteen minutes. Add seasonings such as pepper, salt, garlic powder, and dried herbs to taste.

A serving of one and a half cups of soup per person is a good rule of thumb. Float a few flourless croutons (see page 128) on top for added texture and flavor.

## Make Your Own Stock

You purists out there can make your own vegetable, beef, chicken, or fish stock pretty easily, which will not have the salt and preservatives found in canned stock. Combine solid ingredients (read "leftovers") with as much water. Season with a bay leaf and whole black peppercorns if you like. Bring this mixture to a boil and then reduce the heat and simmer about an hour. Allow the stock to cool and then strain out the solids. With meat and fish stock, once the stock has cooled, place it in the refrigerator for a couple of hours and the extra fat will rise to the top, making it easy to skim off. Freeze the stock in convenient-size containers for later use.

## Cold Remedy

For a different twist on a cold day, consider ginger-coriander lentil soup. Some packaged dried lentils require soaking, while others don't. Follow the directions. When the lentils are ready, place 2 cups of them into your blender. Add about ½ cup diced carrots and ½ cup chopped onions—the quantities need not be exact—and blend until the mixture is almost pureed, leaving it thick and hearty. Add freshly grated ginger and coriander to taste. By the way, once you try fresh ginger, you'll appreciate the difference from that ginger you purchase in a glass container or spice can and you'll never use anything else!

Heat the blended mixture without boiling. The appetizing aroma from the combination of ginger and coriander will fill your kitchen and will delight your family and guests. A cup of this soup is great for lunch, while a bowl at dinnertime, served with a tossed green salad, will provide a healthful, nutrient-rich meal you can be proud was prepared from scratch. Simply sit back and accept the compliments.

## Chill Out on a Hot Day

A warm day need not keep you from serving soup and salad for lunch or dinner. In fact, if you serve a delicious chilled soup, your family or guests may consider it a stroke of genius.

Serve a simple chilled tomato bouillon made with sugar-free tomato juice. To make this, combine 2 cups tomato juice, 1 small onion, and 1 celery stalk, both finely chopped. Spice it up with a bay leaf, cloves, basil, and fennel. Let the mixture sit 1 hour, then heat to boiling. Reduce heat and simmer 10 minutes. Allow to cool, then refrigerate before serving. Compliment this soup with a crisp spinach salad to bring smiles to the faces of those around your table.

If you are really looking to impress someone, prepare my Two-Tone Melon Soup. When your guests see two colors in one bowl, be prepared to receive the accolades.

If melon isn't a favorite of yours, experiment with other fruits such as pears or peaches with a garnish of blueberries or sliced strawberries. You can also serve two-tone berry soup as a dessert.

Have fun no matter what soup you choose to serve. The options are as far reaching as your imagination allows!

# Cream of Carrot and Potato Soup

*Jean McCaugherty, Lincoln, Nebraska*

This hearty dish will tempt the taste buds and leave you feeling satisfied.

2 tablespoons butter
½ cup finely chopped onion
1 pound carrots, shredded
1 pound potatoes, shredded
6 cups chicken broth
¹/₃ teaspoon dried thyme
½ teaspoon Tabasco sauce
1 bay leaf
Salt and black pepper to taste
1½ cups milk
1 to 2 cups shredded cheddar cheese
Fresh parsley, for garnish

Sauté butter and onion in large pot.

Add carrots, potatoes, chicken broth, thyme, Tabasco, bay leaf, and salt and pepper. Simmer until tender.

Add milk and cheese and stir until cheese is melted. Remove and discard bay leaf. Sprinkle each serving with fresh parsley. Enjoy.

*Serves 6 to 8*

# Italian Vegetable Soup

*Jean Rouse, Independence, Iowa*

This soup can be used as an entrée when combined with a side salad and light dessert.

1 pound Italian sausage or ground beef
1 cup diced onion
1 cup sliced celery
1 cup sliced carrot
2 cloves garlic, minced
One 15-ounce can red kidney beans, drained
One 15-ounce can black beans, drained
2 cups water
5 teaspoons beef bouillon granules
1 tablespoon dried parsley flakes
One 16-ounce can diced tomatoes
One 15-ounce can tomato sauce
½ teaspoon salt
½ teaspoon dried oregano
½ teaspoon dried sweet basil
½ teaspoon black pepper
2½ cups shredded cabbage
1 cup Parmesan cheese, for garnish

Brown meat in heavy pot and drain. Add all ingredients except cabbage and cheese and bring to boil. Lower heat, cover, and simmer 20 minutes. Add cabbage and simmer until tender, 5 to 10 minutes. Sprinkle with cheese before serving.

*Serves 8*

# Creamy Tomato Soup

Creamy tomato soup is excellent for a cold, blustery day. The baking soda and Splenda in this dish reduce the acidity of the tomatoes. You can add a garnish of marinated silken tofu, rolled in cornmeal and baked for crispness.

Three 15-ounce cans diced tomatoes
1 cup chicken broth
½ cup cream or milk
¼ teaspoon baking soda
1 individual packet Splenda
½ teaspoon salt
1 teaspoon black pepper

Simmer tomatoes and broth 15 minutes. Stir in cream, baking soda, Splenda, salt, and pepper. Stir well and simmer until hot. Using stick blender (or pour into regular blender), mix until smooth and creamy. Serve.

*Serves 2 to 3*

# Two-Tone Melon Soup

This is a party-friendly soup. Your guests will be impressed to see two separate soups in one bowl. You can also keep it simple and leave out the raspberries and melon balls, and instead garnish it with fresh mint leaves.

1 ripe cantaloupe, seeded and diced
1 tablespoon lemon juice
4 tablespoons nonfat plain yogurt
½ honeydew melon, seeded and diced
1 tablespoon lime juice
1 teaspoon minced fresh mint
½ honeydew melon, seeded and scooped into balls with
    melon baller
½ pint raspberries

In blender, puree the cantaloupe, lemon juice, and 2 tablespoons yogurt. Transfer to covered container and refrigerate at least 3 hours.

Wash blender, then puree honeydew, lime juice, remaining yogurt, and mint. Transfer to covered container and refrigerate at least 3 hours.

To serve, put the 2 melon purees into separate pitchers. With 1 pitcher in each hand, pour soups simultaneously into each soup bowl. The two soups will stay separated.

Garnish honeydew side with raspberries and cantaloupe side with honeydew balls.

*Serves 6*

# Dilled Cucumber Yogurt Soup

This soup may be served hot or cold. It is perfect for parties and makes a very elegant brunch dish.

3 cups peeled, seeded, and chopped cucumber
2 tablespoons snipped fresh dill
2 tablespoons balsamic vinegar
1 cup chicken broth
4 cups nonfat plain yogurt
½ teaspoon salt
¼ teaspoon black pepper
Radish slices, for garnish
Fresh dill sprigs, for garnish

Combine cucumber, dill, vinegar, and broth in blender or food processor. Work in batches, if necessary. Add yogurt and blend until smooth. Season with salt and pepper.

To serve hot, pour into medium saucepan and heat over low until warm. Do not boil.

To serve cold, pour into covered container and refrigerate at least 2 hours.

Ladle hot or chilled soup into bowls and garnish with radish slices and dill sprigs.

*Serves 6*

# Turkey and Barley Soup

This colorful dish is easy to prepare and the barley makes for a hearty soup that is a meal in itself.

1 pound ground turkey
One 15-ounce can diced tomatoes
½ cup chopped celery
1 cup uncooked barley
1 large carrot, chopped
2 medium zucchini, sliced
1 bay leaf
2 tablespoons dried parsley
2 chicken bouillon cubes
8 cups water

Brown turkey over medium-high heat in large skillet. Combine all ingredients in large pot and simmer, covered, 1½ hours before serving.

*Serves 6*

# Chicken Vegetable Soup

The best chicken soup is the one you make yourself. You can control the flavor by adding your favorite ingredients. The next time you roast a chicken or get a deli rotisserie chicken, save the leftovers (meat and bones) to make this simple soup. The addition of red wine makes a more flavorful stock.

1 or 2 chickens' leftovers
2 celery stalks, chopped
2 carrots, chopped
1 onion, slivered
2 to 3 cloves garlic, chopped
2 tablespoons black pepper
1 tablespoon salt
½ cup dry red wine
Water to cover

Place chicken in cheesecloth for easy removal. Put all ingredients in large stockpot. Bring to a boil for 10 minutes. Reduce heat and simmer, covered, 1 hour, skimming top every 10 minutes. Remove chicken and let cool. Separate meat and place back into soup. Serve.

*Serves 4 to 6*

# Cuban Black Bean Soup

This soup can be made into a main course simply by adding more chorizo, a type of sausage found in most grocery stores. Ask your butcher if you cannot find it in the cooler. If you prefer a chunky soup, skip the blending step.

Cooking spray, for coating
1 medium onion, chopped
1 carrot, finely diced
1 red or green bell pepper, diced
2 cloves garlic, minced
1 teaspoon salt
¼ teaspoon black pepper
½ teaspoon ground cumin
4 cups 99 percent fat-free chicken broth
Two 15-ounce cans black beans, drained and rinsed
½ cup sherry
¼ pound chorizo, crumbled (¾ pound for main course)

Coat large stockpot with cooking spray. Sauté onion, carrot, bell pepper, and garlic over medium heat until soft but not browned. Season with salt, pepper, and cumin. Add 2 cups broth and 1 can beans. Simmer 20 minutes, or until vegetables are very tender. Add sherry and puree by batches in blender or use stick blender in pot. In skillet, cook chorizo until browned. Drain well. Add to pot along with remaining broth and beans. Heat through before serving.

*Serves 6 to 8 as a first course, 4 as a main course*

# Split Pea Soup

For a creamy version of this traditional soup, blend it before adding the ham.

One 16-ounce bag split peas
2 medium carrots, chopped
1 large potato, chopped
1 small onion, slivered
1 large ham bone
½ teaspoon black pepper
Water to cover
½ cup chopped ham steak (optional)

Rinse peas. In large stockpot, combine peas, carrots, potato, onion, ham bone (covered in cheesecloth for easier removal), and pepper and cover with water. Bring to a boil. Reduce heat and simmer, covered, about 1½ hours or until vegetables are tender, stirring occasionally to be sure peas don't stick or scorch. Add more water during cooking if soup becomes too thick. Remove ham bone and cool. Separate meat from bone. Add ham to pot and serve.

*Serves 8*

# Potato-Leek Soup

If you chill this, it becomes the classic cold French vichyssoise. If you desire, serve it with warm flourless rolls.

Cooking spray, for coating
4 cups thinly sliced leeks, white part only, thoroughly washed
4 cups peeled and diced potatoes
3 cups 99 percent fat-free chicken broth
Dash of ground nutmeg
1 teaspoon salt
Pinch of white pepper
3 to 4 cups nonfat milk
2 tablespoons chopped fresh chives

Spray medium saucepan with cooking spray. Sauté leeks over medium heat 5 minutes, or until tender but not brown. Add potatoes, broth, nutmeg, salt, and pepper. Bring to a boil, reduce heat, and simmer about 30 minutes, or until potatoes are tender. Puree in batches in blender or with stick blender.

For hot soup, add milk and simmer until warm. For cold soup, stir in milk, cover, and refrigerate until chilled.

To serve, ladle into bowls and garnish with chives.

*Serves 6*

# Mexican Tortilla Soup

Be sure to use tortillas made with corn, not corn flour. This soup is a great alternative for taco and burrito lovers.

2 tablespoons extra virgin olive oil
2 cloves garlic, smashed but not chopped

Four 6-inch corn tortillas (made from corn, not corn flour), cut
    into narrow strips (about 1" x ¼" inch)
1 medium onion, diced
1 red bell pepper, diced
½ teaspoon chili powder
1 medium carrot, diced
1 teaspoon salt
¼ teaspoon black pepper
2 cups 99 percent fat-free chicken
    broth
1 cup tomato or vegetable juice
1 bay leaf
One 15-ounce can red kidney
    beans, drained and rinsed
1 teaspoon lime juice

> *"I have lost forty-five pounds on Dr. Gott's No Flour, No Sugar Diet. For me, the diet is easy."*
>
> Neil, Groveton, Texas

In skillet, heat oil and garlic over medium heat until lightly browned. Remove and discard garlic, reserving oil. Fry tortilla strips in flavored oil, turning often to brown lightly. When strips are golden, 2 to 3 minutes, remove to drain on paper towels.

Drain excess oil from pan. Sauté onion, bell pepper, and chili powder until onion is soft but not browned. Add carrot, salt, and pepper and cook additional 2 to 3 minutes.

Pour mixture into medium saucepan. Add broth, tomato juice, and bay leaf. Simmer 15 minutes. Stir in beans and lime juice. Heat thoroughly.

Discard bay leaf. Divide soup into 4 bowls and garnish each with ¼ of tortilla strips.

*Serves 4*

# Creamy Vegetable Soup

The "cream" in this soup is actually evaporated skim milk and a little cheddar cheese. This gives you a rich, creamy flavor without all the fat and calories.

Cooking spray, for coating
½ onion, diced
9 cloves garlic, peeled and left whole
1 large bunch broccoli, chopped
3 medium carrots, diced
2 medium yellow-fleshed potatoes, diced but not peeled
1 teaspoon salt
½ teaspoon black pepper
One 28-ounce can chopped tomatoes, with juice
3 cups 99 percent fat-free chicken broth, plus more for
      thinning (optional)
2 bay leaves
1 teaspoon dried basil
½ cup red wine
2 cups evaporated skim milk, plus more for thinning
      (optional)
1 cup shredded cheddar cheese

Coat stockpot with cooking spray. Sauté onion and garlic over medium heat. Add broccoli, carrots, potatoes, salt, pepper, and tomatoes with juice. Add broth, bring to a boil, cover, and reduce heat. Simmer ½ hour, or until vegetables are very tender. Puree in batches in blender or use stick blender. Add bay leaves, basil, and wine and simmer 10 minutes. Remove bay leaves. Stir in milk and cheese. Heat until warmed through. Do not boil. Thin with more milk or broth, if desired. Serve.

*Serves 6*

# Clam Chowder

If you like a thick, rich chowder, here's a dish that's sure to please. Potato flakes eliminate the need for flour to thicken the soup.

2 slices bacon, chopped
½ medium onion, diced
1 clove garlic, minced
1 medium carrot, diced
2 medium potatoes, diced
2 cups 99 percent fat-free chicken broth
1 teaspoon salt
½ teaspoon black pepper
4 to 5 cups nonfat milk
Two 6-ounce cans clams, with juice
1 tablespoon dried parsley
½ cup instant potato flakes

In large stockpot, sauté bacon until crisp. Remove and drain on paper towels. Drain bacon grease from pot, leaving just film with which to cook vegetables. Add onion and garlic to pot and sauté over medium heat until soft but not browned. Add carrot, potatoes, and broth. Season with salt and pepper. Bring to a boil and simmer 15 minutes, or until vegetables are tender. Add milk, clams and their juice, and parsley. Do not boil. Stir potato flakes into soup. It will take a few minutes for flakes to rehydrate. Add additional flakes to thicken more, if desired. Just before serving, add crispy bacon pieces.

Variation: For corn chowder, use 2 cups thawed frozen corn in place of 2 cans clams.

*Serves 6*

## Chinese Egg Drop Soup

This is one of the simplest soups around. It's also tasty, low fat, and full of protein. While most tamari sauces contain wheat and sugar, there are some varieties made of just fermented soybeans and salt. Be sure to check the label.

    4 cups 99-percent fat-free chicken broth
    4 eggs, beaten
    1 teaspoon tamari sauce
    One 6-ounce can water chestnuts, chopped
    2 teaspoons chopped green onion, for garnish

Heat broth over high heat to boiling. While stirring boiling broth, pour in eggs. Continue to stir as eggs cook into streamer shapes. Stir in tamari sauce and water chestnuts and heat thoroughly. Ladle soup into bowls and garnish with green onion.

*Serves 4*

## Mushroom Barley Soup

Mushrooms and barley complement each other making this a tasty combination. Barley makes any soup heartier. To turn this into an entrée, add two cups of chopped cooked chicken and serve with a tossed green salad.

    Cooking spray, to coat
    1 leek, rinsed well and chopped
    2 cloves garlic, minced
    1 pound button mushrooms, sliced
    6 cups 99 percent fat-free chicken broth
    ½ cup pearl barley, rinsed

1 medium carrot, diced

½ teaspoon ground oregano

1 teaspoon salt

½ teaspoon black pepper

⅛ teaspoon cayenne pepper

2 tablespoons sherry (optional)

Coat large stockpot with cooking spray. Cook leek and garlic over medium heat until tender but not browned. Add mushrooms and cook until liquid is released, about 5 minutes. Add broth, barley, carrot, oregano, salt, pepper, and cayenne. Bring to a boil, then cover and reduce heat. Simmer about 40 minutes until barley is tender. Add sherry and cook about 5 minutes more, uncovered, before serving.

*Serves 6*

**13**

# *Salads*

Talk about versatile! You can take nearly as many liberties with a salad as you like and still come up with a tasty, healthful addition to your diet. Salads can be served as appetizers, as side dishes, or as the main dish. They work for dinners, lunches, and snacks. Some are even suitable for breakfasts. And for those hard-to-stay-on-my-diet trips out to eat, consider ordering from the many salad variations most restaurants now serve. Even the fast-food restaurants are getting on board, offering some surprisingly good salads.

## Do-It-at-Home Salad Bar

You can have a nightly salad bar for your family by stocking their favorite salad ingredients and letting everyone make his or her own. Start by preparing salad tidbits and storing them in a collection of plastic containers. When dinnertime arrives, just pop the tops off the containers and line them up on the kitchen counter. Invite your family to help themselves. When everyone has finished eating, snap the tops back on the containers and put them away for the next time. This same system also works if you are going to dine alone. You'll be surprised how much more likely you are to eat a healthful salad if all it takes is to open a few containers.

If company is coming over, just serve the ingredients in nicer bowls (then put the leftovers back in their plastic containers). Along with the salad goodies, offer an assortment of lettuces. Break up a few different types ahead of time and store them in zipper bags or buy one or two of the already bagged lettuces available at most supermarkets. Below is a short list of items you may wish to include in your salad bar—the choices are endless.

- Sunflower seeds
- Fresh spinach
- Broccoli and cauliflower florets
- Sliced or baby carrots
- Chopped purple cabbage
- Hearts of palm
- Chopped green onion
- Dried cranberries
- Marinated artichoke hearts
- Fresh mushrooms
- Raisins
- Bamboo shoots
- Bacon bits
- Kidney beans
- Chickpeas
- Apple or pear wedges
- Mandarin orange segments
- Grapefruit segments
- Chopped pineapple
- Seedless grapes
- Cherry tomatoes
- Slices of bell pepper
- Cucumber
- Bean or alfalfa sprouts

## Dressings

Most of the calories from a typical salad come from the dressing, so be wary. Read labels for sugar and fat contents when buying bottled dressings. Most dressings contain sugar. Consider making your own dressing so you can be more in control of what you are eating or look for nonfat or low-fat choices. Dressings can be as simple as the juice of a freshly squeezed lemon or a couple spoonfuls of robust wine vinegar mixed with a little olive oil. Add a teaspoon of sugar-free mustard for additional zing.

Balsamic wine vinegar with olive oil is an excellent combination and it tastes great with salads that include fruits such as pears, strawberries, and orange slices.

Worried about using too much oil? Olive oil, while technically a fat, is a healthful choice. Combine vinegar or lemon juice with oil and spritz your salad with a pump sprayer. This will allow you to control the amount of dressing you use. Each pump of the spritzer is said to add a single calorie.

One of my favorite dressings is Creamy Pesto Dressing that blends yogurt, garlic, basil, and other tasty things for a unique change you'll enjoy. It's simple to prepare.

## Got to Have Croutons?

Most croutons, of course, are a no-no on my No Flour, No Sugar Diet, but you can make you own from one of the flourless breads now available at many stores. Lightly toast the bread, cut it into bite-size pieces, spray or brush them with olive oil, sprinkle with garlic salt, parsley, basil, or oregano, and bake at 225 degrees until browned and crispy (about 8 minutes). Voilà! Delicious flourless croutons.

Another suggestion for crispy croutons is to make them from tofu. You will need a package of extra-firm tofu cut into cubes, 1 tablespoon minced fresh parsley, and 1 cup cornmeal. Marinate the cubes in a sugar-free salad dressing of your choice for ½ hour, roll them in the cornmeal-parsley mixture, and place them on a cookie sheet coated with cooking spray. Bake about 10 minutes in a 350-degree oven for a taste-tempting treat to add to any salad.

If you aren't already, think "salads." They are healthful, inexpensive, and versatile.

# Nanette's Salad

*Nanette Reding, Tulsa, Oklahoma*

This salad not only looks good but is full of healthful nutrients and flavor. Serve it with Nanette's Salad Dressing.

1 medium head Bibb lettuce
4 green onions, chopped
1 avocado, sliced
1 Granny Smith apple, sliced
¼ cup dried cranberries
½ cup crumbled blue cheese
½ cup slivered almonds
1 can sugar-free mandarin oranges, drained

Toss all ingredients together and serve dressed.

*Serves 4*

# Nanette's Salad Dressing

The refreshing taste of this dressing will delight your guests.

½ cup canola oil
2 tablespoons red wine vinegar
2 tablespoons balsamic vinegar
1 tablespoon plain yogurt
1 teaspoon garlic powder
1 teaspoon garlic salt
Black pepper to taste

Mix all ingredients together and pour over Nanette's Salad.

*Serves 4*

# Sugar-Free Grape Salad

*Dottie W. Henson, LaGrange, Georgia*

Making this salad moist and creamy improves the flavor of the Splenda and SugarTwin.

4 to 5 cups red seedless grapes, washed and dried
8 ounces cream cheese, softened
8 ounces sour cream
1½ cups Splenda
1 teaspoon vanilla flavoring
1 teaspoon maple flavoring
Enough milk to make creamy (¼ to ½ cup)
1 cup pecans
1 tablespoon SugarTwin

In large bowl, mix grapes, cream cheese, sour cream, Splenda, flavorings, and milk together. Sprinkle with pecans and SugarTwin. Cover and refrigerate at least 2 hours before serving.

*Serves 4 to 5*

# Avocado Black Bean Salad

*Eileen Mendyka, Anderson, South Carolina*

This salad can be prepared ahead of time, holding well in the refrigerator. Add the avocado right before serving, as it browns quickly when exposed to the air. Chopped chicken or turkey can also be added to make this into a "dinner" salad.

One 15-ounce can black beans, drained and rinsed
1 ripe avocado, seeded, peeled, and chopped
½ pint cherry or grape tomatoes, halved
1 to 2 tablespoons chopped fresh herbs (basil, cilantro, chives, or parsley)
1 tablespoon fresh lime juice
1 tablespoon olive oil
Salt and black pepper to taste

Put all ingredients in bowl and gently stir with wooden spoon.

*Serves 4*

# Chicken Salad with Melon

This is a tasty, colorful dish to consider for special luncheons. The ingredients can be prepared in advance and assembled in no time.

3 cups chopped cooked skinless, boneless chicken
½ cup chopped celery
¼ cup chopped walnuts
½ cup red seedless grapes
½ cup sugar-free vanilla yogurt
¼ cup sugar-free mayonnaise
Salt and black pepper to taste
1 cantaloupe or honeydew melon
4 large lettuce leaves
Fresh chives, for garnish

Combine chicken, celery, walnuts, and grapes in large bowl. In separate bowl, blend yogurt, mayonnaise, salt, and pepper. Add to chicken mixture. Cover and refrigerate.

Trim stem ends of melon and discard. Cut balance of melon into 6 rings. Scoop out seeds and cut off rind, being careful not to break rings. Place 1 lettuce leaf on each plate and top with melon slice. Fill center with chicken salad. Garnish with fresh chives.

*Serves 6*

# Cabbage Salad with Garlic Lemon Dressing

The cabbage in this dish is flavored with fresh lemon juice, giving it a delightful tangy flavor. This is a healthful alternative to traditional coleslaw which usually contains mayonnaise.

1 pound cabbage, thinly sliced
2 green onions, diagonally sliced
1 carrot, coarsely shredded
1 tablespoon chopped fresh flat-leaf parsley
¼ cup extra virgin olive oil
3 tablespoons fresh lemon juice
1 teaspoon grated lemon zest
1 clove garlic, crushed
½ teaspoon salt
Black pepper to taste

Toss cabbage, green onions, carrot, and parsley in large bowl.

In separate small bowl, whisk olive oil, lemon juice, lemon zest, garlic, salt, and pepper. Add dressing to cabbage mixture and toss until coated. Chill, covered, until ready to serve.

*Serves 8*

# Basic Tossed Salad

A salad can be as plain or fancy as you wish it to be. You can replace the lettuce with spinach for a different twist, or add chopped red bell pepper and green onion.

4 cups romaine lettuce, rinsed and patted dry
½ medium cucumber, peeled and thinly sliced
1 medium tomato, diced

½ cup shredded carrot
1/3 cup dressing of your choice

Combine romaine, cucumber, tomato, and carrot in bowl. Pour dressing over top, toss to coat, and serve.

*Serves 4*

# Waldorf Salad

Apples, raisins, and walnuts make this kid-friendly salad full of tasty, fun ingredients. The nonfat yogurt makes it a healthful dish.

2 medium apples of your choice, cored and diced
1 tablespoon plus 2 teaspoons lemon juice
½ cup thinly sliced celery
¼ cup raisins
¼ cup chopped walnuts
1 cup torn lettuce, rinsed and dried
4 tablespoons nonfat plain yogurt
1 tablespoon unsweetened apple juice concentrate

In medium bowl, toss diced apples with 1 tablespoon lemon juice. Add celery, raisins, walnuts, and lettuce and toss until well combined. In small bowl, mix yogurt, remaining lemon juice, and apple juice concentrate. Pour over salad and toss to coat.

*Serves 2*

# "Berry" Fruity Salad

Fruit salads are sweet and delicious. They go with nearly any meal and can even be a dessert. The varieties are limitless and you can create your own by using any fruit you love.

1 pint fresh blueberries, rinsed
1 pint raspberries, rinsed
½ pint blackberries, rinsed
1 cup sliced strawberries
1 cup chunked fresh pineapple
1 large Golden Delicious apple, cored, peeled, and chopped
1½ cups seeded and chunked watermelon
2 large bananas, peeled and chopped
½ lemon
Splenda to taste

In large bowl, combine fruit except lemon. Squeeze lemon juice over fruit and mix thoroughly. Taste. Add Splenda if fruit is not completely ripe and sweet. Serve.

*Serves 6 to 8*

# Chickpea and Wheat Berry Salad

Chickpeas and wheat berries blend well together. The wheat berries add a bit of crunch and the chickpeas are hearty and filling.

One 15-ounce can chickpeas (garbanzo beans), drained
1 cup wheat berries, rinsed and cooked until al dente (see
    package instructions)
One 7-ounce can diced tomatoes, drained
2 small scallions, chopped
½ cup sliced black olives
4 tablespoons extra virgin olive oil
4 tablespoons red wine vinegar
¼ teaspoon salt
1 teaspoon black pepper
1 teaspoon dry mustard

In bowl, combine chickpeas, wheat berries, tomatoes, scallions, and olives. Set aside. In small bowl, combine oil, vinegar, salt, pepper, and mustard. Mix thoroughly and pour over chickpea–wheat berry mixture. Refrigerate at least 1 hour before serving.

*Serves 4*

> *"After I lost weight on Dr. Gott's No Flour, No Sugar Diet, I put on a pair of shorts for the first time and realized the cellulite in my legs was gone!"*
>
> **Barbara, Whittier, California**

# Broccoli Salad

The yogurt-and-apple-juice dressing lend a sweet flavor to this crunchy salad.

2 cups broccoli florets
1/3 cup chopped red onion
1/3 cup sugar-free dried currants
1/3 cup grated carrot
1/4 cup shredded cheese (cheddar, Colby Jack, etc.)
2 tablespoons chopped pecans
3 tablespoons crumbled bacon
1/3 cup nonfat plain yogurt
1/4 cup sugar-free apple juice concentrate

In bowl, mix broccoli, onion, currants, carrot, cheese, pecans, and bacon. Set aside. In small bowl, mix yogurt and apple juice. Pour over broccoli mixture, cover, and refrigerate 1 hour.

*Serves 4*

# Asian Chicken Slaw

Make this without the chicken for a side dish with dinner. If you choose to use bagged coleslaw mix from the store, be sure to purchase a bag that doesn't include salad dressing.

2 cups thinly shredded cabbage
1 red bell pepper, cut into thin strips
1 cup fresh bean sprouts
1 cup shredded carrots
2 cups diced, cooked chicken
1/2 cup Thai Peanut Dressing (see page 144)

In large bowl, toss vegetables and chicken. Pour dressing over, toss to coat, and serve.

*Serves 3 as a dinner, 6 as a salad course*

# Fruit Salad

You can make this with any combination of fruit you like, including no-sugar-added canned fruit. For a more elegant salad, toss with one-fourth cup unsweetened flaked coconut.

1 large apple, cored and diced (tossed with 2 teaspoons
    lemon juice)
1 large pear, cored and diced
1 large peach, pitted, peeled, and diced
1 large nectarine, pitted and diced
1 cup canned sugar-free pineapple chunks, drained
1 large banana, peeled and sliced
1 cup raisins
½ cup dressing (Creamy Lime Poppy Seed Dressing or Orange
    Poppy Seed Vinaigrette; see page 143)

Place fruit in large bowl and mix. Toss with dressing and serve.

*Serves 8 to 10*

# Potato Salad

Potato salad is an all-American summer side dish. You can make interesting variations depending on what kind of dressing you use. Try Ranch-Style Dressing or Creamy Pesto Dressing (see pages 144 and 145).

2 pounds small red potatoes
Water to cover
1 large celery stalk, chopped
2 hard-cooked eggs, chopped
¼ cup chopped green onion
1 small jar roasted red peppers, drained and chopped
½ cup dressing of your choice

In large saucepan, cover potatoes with water and bring to a boil over medium heat. Cook until potatoes are tender when pierced with knife, about 25 minutes. Drain and cool completely.

If potatoes are very small, leave whole; otherwise cut in half. In large bowl, toss potatoes, celery, eggs, onion, peppers, and dressing. Serve immediately or keep refrigerated.

*Serves 8 to 10*

# Rice Salad

Why should pasta have all the fun? Make a rice salad instead. This is party friendly and sure to please. Using apple juice concentrate instead of the traditional olive oil makes this a lower-fat dressing with a refreshing sweet taste.

2 cups cooked long grain rice
½ cup shredded carrots
1 small apple, cored and diced
¼ cup white wine vinegar
2 tablespoons unsweetened apple juice concentrate
½ teaspoon salt
Bibb lettuce leaves
¼ pound cooked small or medium shrimp
2 tablespoons chopped green onion, for garnish

In medium bowl, combine rice, carrots, and apple. Toss. In small bowl, whisk together vinegar, apple juice, and salt. Stir into rice mixture. Cover and refrigerate at least 1 hour or overnight.

To serve, place 1 or more lettuce leaves (depending on size) on each of 6 plates. Scoop about ½ cup of rice salad onto lettuce. Sprinkle with a few shrimp and garnish with green onion.

*Serves 6*

# Tabouli Salad

Bulgur, the grain called for in this salad, is popular in the Middle East. It is gaining popularity in the United States and is frequently used in vegetarian dishes. (Tabouli salad, too, is becoming more popular.) This recipe is excellent with fresh tomatoes replacing the canned version when ripe, juicy ones are available.

1 cup cracked wheat bulgur, cooked in water according to
     package directions
1 cup canned tomatoes, drained, with liquid reserved
½ cup chopped green onion
1 green bell pepper, chopped
¼ medium cucumber, peeled and chopped
¼ cup sliced black olives
1 tablespoon chopped fresh mint
½ cup chopped fresh parsley
¼ cup fresh lime or lemon juice
¼ cup extra virgin olive oil
½ teaspoon salt
¼ teaspoon black pepper

In large bowl, stir together bulgur, tomatoes, green onion, bell pepper, cucumber, olives, mint, and parsley. In small bowl, whisk together lime or lemon juice, olive oil, salt, and pepper. Pour dressing over tabouli. Cover and refrigerate at least 2 hours to allow flavors to blend before serving.

*Serves 6*

# Dressings

All the dressings here keep well for several days when properly stored.

## Orange Poppy Seed Vinaigrette

The sweet orange and sour vinegar make for a refreshing dressing that is good for fruit or green salads and coleslaw.

⅓ cup orange juice
¼ cup white wine vinegar
3 tablespoons sugar-free Dijon-style mustard
2 tablespoons extra virgin olive oil
1 tablespoon poppy seeds

Mix all ingredients in jar with tight-fitting lid. Shake until well mixed. Let stand for at least ½ hour to blend flavors. Store in covered jar in refrigerator.

*Makes 1 cup*

## Creamy Lime Poppy Seed Dressing

Good for fruit salads and coleslaw. For variation, use a different fruit flavor of yogurt, such as orange, strawberry, lemon, blueberry, or blackberry. Apple cider vinegar is believed by some to have valuable health benefits. It has a delicious flavor that works nicely in salad dressings.

1 cup fat-free, sugar-free lime yogurt
½ teaspoon poppy seeds
1 tablespoon apple cider vinegar

In small bowl, whisk together all ingredients. Let stand for at least ½ hour to blend flavors. Store in covered jar in refrigerator.

*Makes 1 cup*

# Ranch-Style Dressing

This is very good as a dip for raw vegetable sticks and it is a low-calorie version of popular ranch dressing recipes that commonly contain mayonnaise.

1 cup nonfat buttermilk

1 tablespoon sugar-free Dijon-style mustard

2 teaspoons lemon juice

2 teaspoons chopped fresh parsley

½ teaspoon garlic powder

¼ teaspoon dried dill

¼ teaspoon black pepper

Combine all ingredients in jar with tightly fitting lid. Shake until well combined. Let sit ½ hour to allow flavors to blend. Store in covered jar in refrigerator.

Variations: For blue cheese dressing, add ¼ cup crumbled blue cheese. For Southwestern ranch dressing, substitute ½ teaspoon chili powder for the dill.

*Makes about 1 cup*

# Thai Peanut Dressing

This is great for an Asian-style coleslaw or a tossed green salad. It's also good when drizzled on chicken or shrimp.

¼ cup natural or homemade creamy sugar-free peanut butter

¼ cup sugar-free rice wine vinegar

¼ cup orange juice

1 tablespoon tamari sauce

1 clove garlic, minced

½ teaspoon ground or peeled and grated fresh ginger

In small bowl, whisk together all ingredients. Store in an airtight container in refrigerator.

*Makes ¾ cup*

# Creamy Pesto Dressing

This dressing combines the powerful impact of pesto with the creaminess of yogurt for a very flavorful, rich dressing. Great drizzled on sliced cucumbers or a green salad.

½ cup firmly packed fresh basil leaves
½ cup nonfat plain yogurt
¼ cup grated Parmesan cheese
¼ cup pine nuts
1 tablespoon extra virgin olive oil
1 clove garlic, minced
Salt and black pepper to taste

Combine all ingredients except salt and pepper in blender or food processor. Blend until smooth. Season with salt and pepper to taste. Store in covered jar in refrigerator.

*Makes about ¾ cup*

# 14

## Wraps

Wraps are becoming more popular by the day as low-carbohydrate, low-calorie alternatives to sandwiches, burritos, and stuffed pita pockets. Many sandwich shops and restaurants now offer them for lunch and dinner filled with a variety of interesting combinations including chicken, beef, shrimp, feta and other cheeses, avocado, falafel, mushrooms, salsa, and much more. Lettuce and cabbage wraps are a hit in parts of the United States, including the West Coast, as a means of controlling calories, eliminating flour, and providing more nutritious alternatives. Even fast-food chains have joined the effort and offer wraps as a way of making their selection of menu items more extensive. Across the pond, in the UK, the wrap market has grown so substantially in the last couple of years that most major sandwich shops are in on this innovative idea.

### Lower in Calories, Higher in Nutrition

Why are wraps gaining in popularity? Consider that the average slice of white bread contains 80 calories. Assuming you want a full sandwich, you are looking at 160 calories without any filling. One slice of crunchy oat bread (made with flour also) contains 120 calories or 240 for a full sandwich. A medium-size tortilla (made with flour) has 180 calories.

Let's consider what happens when you wrap your favorite lunch-time sandwich fillings in lettuce or cabbage leaves instead of placing them between two pieces of bread. Since two pieces of bread combine for roughly 200 calories and two leaves of lettuce or cabbage contain perhaps 5 calories, with this one move you have eliminated 195 calories from your meal. Thus, the wraps I recommend on the No Flour, No Sugar Diet use lettuce or cabbage leaves instead of a traditional flour wrap (although, you can also make any of these recipes with a no-flour tortilla, available at most stores).

## Everything but the Kitchen Sink

Wraps vary greatly in style and ingredients, offering limitless possibilities. This chapter offers many good wrap recipes, but you don't have to follow them. Be inventive—anything goes. You might spread a leaf of your choice with mustard and fill it with alfalfa sprouts, tomatoes, cucumbers, roasted red peppers, and cold crab. Another choice might be chopped chicken, shredded lettuce, diced tomatoes, and celery, with a dollop of salsa for a spicier flavor.

Nearly any lettuce from iceberg to romaine works. Leaves that are pliable enough to roll but strong enough so they won't rip make the best choices. If you choose to use one of the smaller varieties of lettuce, try putting two leaves together. The leaves of many cabbages are soft enough to use as wraps and others may be lightly steamed to make them pliable. To steam them, place a steamer insert or an upside-down bowl in a pan with an inch or two of water. Place the cabbage in the pan and heat on medium high. Be careful not to overcook the cabbage or it will become limp.

Spreading plain yogurt on a lettuce leaf and filling it with shredded carrot, raisins, sliced celery, and chopped walnuts creates a tasty snack. You will have made an extremely nutrient-rich dish. Garnish your creation with tomato wedges for an extra splash of color.

The Mediterranean Bean Wraps are a party-friendly idea and are filled with good flavor and healthful ingredients. The black olives, cucumber, feta cheese, and navy beans combine to create a dish sure to bring praise from your guests. In addition, like all wraps, they're simple to put together and can be made in advance, allowing you more time for other things in your busy day.

If you're really ready to experiment, consider an Asian wrap with romaine lettuce. Sauté your choice of vegetables in a skillet, then add some diced chicken, tofu, garlic, and the juice from half a small lime. Before filling the romaine, drizzle an Asian sauce, such as my Thai Peanut Dressing, on the leaf for extra flavor.

Should you wish to use soy sauce, try tamari instead. This substitute is slightly thicker but is available wheat free and sugar free, unlike traditional soy sauce. When shopping, be sure to read the ingredients label to ensure it does not contain flour or sugar. This can also replace Worcestershire sauce. Several of the recipes in this chapter as well as in other chapters call for tamari.

There is no limit to the ingredients a wrap can contain. Chopped spinach, ripe avocado, soy nuts, marinated tofu, garlic, onion, eggplant, and leftover vegetables from your refrigerator will combine for a surprisingly pleasant alternative meal. Don't be afraid to experiment. You're sure to find numerous combinations that will blend to your satisfaction. And, your choices will be right far more often than not.

You've probably become used to slipping sandwich fixings between two slices of bread but consider the alternatives in this section. Think healthy; wrap those same ingredients in a lettuce leaf or flour-free crepe and enjoy a truly more healthful meal.

# Flour-Free Crepes

Crepes traditionally offer elegance to any meal. I've included a few excellent crepe wrap recipes in this chapter. Making crepes is easy and at the same time will impress almost any guest. This recipe for flour-free crepes calls for arrowroot powder instead of the traditional flour.

2 eggs
¾ cup nonfat milk
6 tablespoons arrowroot powder
1 teaspoon baking powder
Dash of salt
1 tablespoon extra virgin olive oil
Cooking spray, for coating

In bowl, beat eggs about 2 minutes with electric mixer on medium speed until pale yellow and fluffy. Add in milk, arrowroot, baking powder, salt, and olive oil and continue to mix until well blended.

Coat 12" skillet with cooking spray and warm over medium-low heat. Add 2 tablespoons of mixture to hot skillet and swirl to evenly coat bottom. Cook until lightly browned (in properly heated pan, crepe will take seconds to brown). Then carefully flip crepe with spatula and repeat on second side. Remove from pan and place between layers of waxed paper. Repeat until all batter is used.

*Makes about 6 crepes*

# Taco Wraps

*Joan Krauss, Freeland, Michigan*

Taco fixings in lettuce are an excellent source of nutrient-rich ingredients without added flour.

> *"My husband and I lost forty and sixty pounds respectively with your No Flour, No Sugar Diet. We also now walk twenty-five to thirty-five miles a week and are more active than ever."*
>
> *Sharon, Auburn, Indiana*

1 pound lean ground beef
1 package taco seasoning
½ head lettuce, rinsed and dried
2 large tomatoes, diced
1 medium onion, chopped

Brown beef in frying pan. Drain off any liquid. Add taco seasoning with amount of water indicated on package. Spoon mixture onto lettuce leaves and top with tomatoes and onion. Roll and serve.

*Serves 4*

# Guacamole Wraps

Fresh veggies make this wrap a favorite. Experiment with your own ingredients.

1 large ripe avocado, pit removed and peeled
1 medium tomato, diced
1 teaspoon salt
1 teaspoon black pepper
½ small jalapeño chile, seeded and finely chopped
4 large lettuce leaves, rinsed and dried
4 fresh button mushrooms, chopped
⅓ cup alfalfa sprouts
1 ounce roasted soy nuts

Mash avocado in medium bowl until smooth. Add tomato, salt, pepper, and jalapeño. Spread avocado-tomato mixture down center of each lettuce leaf. Sprinkle on mushrooms, alfalfa sprouts, and soy nuts. Roll and serve.

*Serves 4*

## Wonderful, Versatile Tofu

How often have you walked through your grocery store to see tofu displayed, wondering what on earth it is used for and what it tastes like? If you are like most Americans, you passed on buying it. After all, what would you do with it once you got it home? Well, tofu is very versatile and can successfully be used in salads, wraps, main courses, desserts, and more.

Tofu is a soybean product that is inexpensive and low in calories, fat, and sodium. It contains high concentrations of B vitamins, minerals, calcium, and protein. It is often substituted for meats, cheeses, and some dairy products. It is easy to digest and relatively bland. Its strong suit is that it picks up the flavors of other foods with which it is combined. Since it is cholesterol free, tofu is great for individuals who are concerned about cholesterol in their diets.

Tofu's use in China dates back at least twenty-two hundred years. It is still a dietary staple in Asia. There are three kinds of tofu—silken, soft, and firm.

Silken tofu has the highest moisture content. Its texture is often compared to fine custard. This form is preferred for blending with other foods and is sometimes used in fruit smoothies because of its creamy consistency. It can be used in place of cream cheese. For a no flour, no sugar dessert similar to chocolate pudding, blend silken tofu with unsweetened cocoa powder and an artificial sweetener to taste.

Soft tofu is a bit firmer and becomes an excellent replacement for the pasta used in lasagna or other macaroni dishes.

Firm tofu is often cubed and is used in salads, baked casseroles, and soups. It holds up well in stir-fry recipes and can even be grilled like a steak.

Tofu is commonly sold in packages containing water that keep it moist and allow storage in the refrigerator for up to a week. (Remember to check the sell-by date on the package.) It also stores well for up to a month when frozen.

When you're marinating tofu, it is best to remove as much moisture as possible. That way, it can absorb more of the marinade. To do this, cut the tofu in half lengthwise and place it on a cutting board with a heavy, flat object on top. Tilt the board toward your sink so the moisture can drain. Let it stand for about 30 minutes, then add the marinade and proceed with the recipe.

If you haven't already, expand your horizons and give this unique product a try. The recipes in this book that include tofu as an ingredient are a good place to start.

# Marinated Tofu Wraps

Tofu makes an excellent wrap when marinated in chili sauce.

14 ounces firm or extra-firm tofu
¼ cup sugar-free chili sauce
Cooking spray, for coating
Sugar-free yellow mustard
4 Flour-Free Crepes (see page 149)

Cut tofu into 2 layers (much like cake) and slice each layer in half, creating 4 "blocks." Toss tofu in chili sauce and marinate 1 hour. Preheat frying pan coated with cooking spray. Remove tofu from chili sauce and place in frying pan. Cook 10 to 15 minutes, turning once, until golden brown. Spread mustard on crepes and place marinated tofu on top. Wrap crepes around tofu and serve.

*Serves 4*

# Cashew Crepes

The zippy ingredients in this recipe will be a delight. They make a great crunchy midday meal.

2 tablespoons extra virgin olive oil
1 small yellow onion, minced
2 cloves garlic, chopped
1 tablespoon peeled and grated fresh ginger
1½ cups chopped celery
¾ cup chopped cashews
4 tablespoons tamari sauce
1 individual packet Splenda
6 Flour-Free Crepes (see page 149)

Coat frying pan with olive oil and sauté onion, garlic, and ginger until soft, about 5 minutes. Add celery to pan and stir-fry 10 to 15 minutes over medium-high heat, stirring constantly. Lower heat to medium low and add cashews, stirring 3 minutes more. Remove from heat. Mix in the tamari and Splenda.

Lay out crepes and fill evenly with mixture. Roll and serve.

*Serves 6*

# Veggie-Ham Wraps

This fresh veggie wrap is filled with colorful, crunchy ingredients sure to please. Because they are small, place two or three wraps on each plate.

6 celery stalks
2 carrots
12 medium-size lettuce leaves, rinsed and dried
6 tablespoons plain yogurt
½ cup alfalfa sprouts
6 thin slices deli ham, halved
1 cup sugar-free salsa

Cut celery stalks crosswise in half or thirds. Cut carrots into similar-length pieces. Then cut lengthwise in quarters.

Lay out lettuce leaves. Spread ½ tablespoon yogurt onto the center of each lettuce leaf. Fill celery stalks with small amount of alfalfa sprouts and place carrot on top of sprouts. Wrap ½ slice ham around each filled celery stalk. Place celery in center of lettuce leaf. Roll and serve with side of salsa for dipping.

*Serves 4 to 6*

# Turkey Wraps

This wrap is rich and satisfying and the turkey is a great source of protein.

6 tablespoons low-fat cream cheese
6 large lettuce leaves, rinsed and dried
6 thin slices deli turkey
½ cucumber, diced
1 large tomato, diced
½ cup alfalfa sprouts
1½ cups sugar-free salsa

Spread 1 tablespoon cream cheese on each lettuce leaf and fill evenly with turkey, cucumber, tomato, and alfalfa sprouts. Roll and serve with salsa as a dip.

*Serves 6*

# Spicy Tofu Wraps

Some cabbages, such as the napa variety, have tender leaves that make them excellent for wraps. Cabbage is also an excellent choice for Asian-inspired wrap ingredients such as this dish.

1 package extra-firm tofu, drained and diced
Salt and black pepper to taste
Red pepper flakes to taste
Cooking spray, for coating
3 cloves garlic, chopped
1 tablespoon peeled and grated fresh ginger
2 cups chopped shiitake mushrooms
3 tablespoons sugar-free Dijon-style mustard
6 large cabbage leaves, rinsed and dried
3 medium tomatoes, cut into wedges, for garnish

Preheat oven to 350 degrees.

Spread tofu on cookie sheet and sprinkle with salt, pepper, and red pepper flakes. Bake 30 minutes.

Over medium-high heat, preheat frying pan coated with cooking spray. Sauté garlic and ginger 5 minutes. Add mushrooms and cook another 10 minutes. Add tofu and sauté 3 or 4 minutes longer.

Spread mustard on each cabbage leaf and fill evenly with tofu mixture. Roll and serve with tomato wedges.

*Serves 6*

# Tasty Chicken Wraps

Leftover chicken makes an excellent main ingredient for this wrap.

3 cups diced, cooked, skinless, boneless chicken
½ cup chopped celery
1 small red onion, chopped
¼ cup chopped walnuts
1 tablespoon dried parsley
3 tablespoons sugar-free mayonnaise
6 large lettuce leaves, rinsed and dried
Sugar-free mustard
2 medium tomatoes, cut into wedges, for garnish
1 small cucumber, sliced, for garnish

Combine chicken, celery, onion, walnuts, parsley, and mayonnaise in bowl. Stir until well blended. Spread lettuce leaves with light coating of mustard. Fill with chicken mixture. Roll and serve with tomato wedges and cucumber slices.

*Serves 6*

# Mediterranean Bean Wraps

This flavorful recipe includes protein-packed beans. The feta cheese, basil, and lime juice add a touch of zing.

One 15-ounce can navy beans, drained and rinsed
¼ medium cucumber, peeled and minced
¼ cup chopped green onion
1 tablespoon julienned fresh basil
¼ cup sliced black olives
2 tablespoons extra virgin olive oil
2 tablespoons fresh lime juice
¼ teaspoon salt
⅛ teaspoon black pepper
6 large leaves lettuce, rinsed and dried
4 ounces crumbled feta cheese, for garnish
1 medium tomato, diced, for garnish

In medium bowl, mix beans, cucumber, onion, basil, and olives. In small bowl, whisk together oil, lime juice, salt, and pepper. Pour dressing over bean mixture and stir to coat. Scoop equal amounts of bean mixture onto lettuce leaves and wrap to secure filling. Garnish with cheese and tomato and serve.

*Serves 6*

## Curried Tuna Wraps

The curry and cream cheese give this tuna a creamy, exotic flavor. For a sweet twist, add a tablespoon of raisins to each wrap before rolling, or use raisins as a garnish.

One 6-ounce can tuna in water, drained
4 ounces low-fat cream cheese, softened
½ teaspoon curry powder
¼ teaspoon black pepper
6 lettuce leaves, rinsed and dried

In a medium bowl, mix tuna, cream cheese, curry powder, and pepper. Blend well. Divide mixture among the 6 lettuce leaves. Roll and serve.

*Serves 3*

## Green Acres Wraps

This is a creamy, flavorful way to eat spinach. The eggs make for a hearty wrap.

Cooking spray, for coating
One 10-ounce package fresh baby spinach
1 teaspoon garlic salt
½ teaspoon black pepper
4 hard-cooked eggs, chopped
¼ cup nonfat plain yogurt
1 tablespoon minced fresh chives
1 tablespoon lemon juice
2 teaspoons sugar-free Dijon-style mustard
6 lettuce leaves, rinsed and dried

Coat skillet with cooking spray.

Heat spinach over medium-high heat until lightly wilted, 2 or 3 minutes, tossing with wooden spoon or spatula. Remove from heat. Drain spinach thoroughly and chop. Season with garlic salt and pepper. Stir in eggs, yogurt, chives, lemon juice, and mustard. Mix well. Spoon onto lettuce leaves, roll, and serve.

*Serves 3*

## Shrimp Caesar Wraps

This is a shrimp Caesar salad that you can hold in your hand. These wraps make a great finger food for parties.

Cooking spray, for coating
½ corn tortilla (made with corn, not corn flour), cut into
    narrow strips
½ pound small shrimp, cooked
¼ cup sugar-free Caesar dressing (be sure to check the
    ingredients label)
4 romaine lettuce leaves, rinsed and dried

Coat skillet with cooking spray. Fry tortilla strips over medium-high heat about 5 minutes, turning occasionally, until crispy. Remove from heat and set aside. In medium bowl, mix shrimp with dressing. Spoon onto romaine leaves. Sprinkle with tortilla strips. Roll and serve.

*Serves 2*

# Reuben Wraps

Love Reuben sandwiches? Try this no-flour version.

4 ounces low-fat cream cheese, softened
2 tablespoons sugar-free Russian dressing (be sure to check
    the ingredients label)
¼ pound chopped corned beef
¼ cup grated Swiss cheese
2 tablespoons sauerkraut, drained
8 Flour-Free Crepes (see page 149)

Preheat oven to 350 degrees.

In medium bowl, mix together cream cheese, dressing, corned beef, cheese, and sauerkraut. Scoop onto center of crepes and roll up. Place on baking sheet and bake 10 minutes, or until filling is warm and cheese is melted.

*Serves 4*

# Lox Wraps

There is nothing like the flavor of smoked salmon to whet the appetite. These wraps make excellent hors d'oeuvres.

4 ounces low-fat cream cheese, softened
4 lettuce leaves, rinsed and dried
1 tablespoon drained capers
8 thin slices lox
2 thin slices onion, halved
2 medium plum tomatoes, quartered, for garnish

Spread 1 ounce cream cheese on each lettuce leaf. Sprinkle with capers, then lay 2 slices lox and ½ slice onion on each. Roll and serve with tomato wedges.

*Serves 2*

# Philly Cheese Steak Wraps

This is another no-flour version of a favorite sandwich.

Cooking spray, for coating
½ red bell pepper, sliced
1 slice onion, cut in half
4 slices provolone cheese
4 lettuce leaves, rinsed and dried
8 thin slices deli roast beef

Coat skillet with cooking spray and place over medium-high heat. Sauté bell pepper and onion until tender, about 5 minutes.

Lay 1 slice cheese on each lettuce leaf followed by ¼ of vegetable mixture. Top with 2 slices roast beef. Roll and serve.

*Serves 4*

# Ham and Egg Salad

This is a heartier twist on traditional egg salad.

4 hard-cooked eggs, chopped
½ cup finely diced lean ham
1 tablespoon nonfat plain yogurt
1 teaspoon sugar-free Dijon-style mustard
2 teaspoons dill pickle relish
¼ teaspoon black pepper
Dash of cayenne pepper
4 romaine lettuce leaves, rinsed and dried
½ melon of your choice, seeded, peeled, and sliced, for
    garnish

In small bowl, mix all ingredients except romaine and melon until well blended. Spoon onto romaine leaves. Roll and serve with melon slices.

*Serves 2*

# Island Chicken Salad Wraps

The pineapple in this recipe introduces a tropical, refreshing twist to this wrap.

1 cup diced cooked chicken
1 celery stalk, diced
¼ cup canned sugar-free crushed pineapple, drained
3 ounces low-fat cream cheese, softened
4 corn tortillas (made with corn, not corn flour)
½ cup lettuce, rinsed, dried, and shredded

In medium bowl, mix chicken, celery, pineapple, and cream cheese until well blended. Heat tortillas, 1 at a time, in dry skillet, turning until warm. Divide chicken mixture among tortillas and top with shredded lettuce. Roll and serve.

*Serves 4*

# Potato Tacos

These unusual tacos will surely delight your taste buds. The potatoes make for a hearty version.

½ pound lean ground turkey
1 cup diced cooked potato
1 teaspoon chili powder
½ teaspoon salt
⅛ teaspoon black pepper
½ cup sugar-free salsa
4 corn tortillas (made with corn, not corn flour)
½ cup shredded cabbage

In skillet over medium-high heat, brown turkey. Drain any fat. Add potato and stir. Season with chili powder, salt, and pepper. Blend in salsa and cook until some of salsa juice evaporates.

Heat tortillas, 1 at a time, in dry skillet, turning until warm. Divide taco mixture among tortillas and top with cabbage. Roll and serve immediately.

*Serves 4*

# Grilled Mediterranean Vegetable Wraps

If you prefer, you can use four small zucchini in place of the eggplants in this recipe. Both are cooked and assembled the same way. Or for a heartier wrap, use the same amounts of both eggplant and zucchini.

> 2 Japanese eggplants, cut lengthwise into 6 slices
> Cooking spray, for coating
> Dash of salt
> 3 slices provolone cheese, cut in half
> 6 Flour-Free Crepes (see page 149)
> 1 small jar roasted red peppers, cut into strips
> ⅓ cup Creamy Pesto Dressing (see page 145)

Light outdoor grill or preheat oven to 375 degrees.

Coat eggplant slices with cooking spray and sprinkle with salt. If grilling outdoors, cook over medium heat, 3 minutes per side. If baking, place eggplant slices on baking sheet and bake 5 minutes per side. Let cool.

Place ½ slice cheese on each crepe. Cover with 1 slice eggplant and several red pepper strips. Drizzle with two teaspoons dressing. Roll and serve.

*Serves 6*

*"I've been on the No Flour, No Sugar Diet now about two months. It is great! I've lost thirty-five pounds and am still losing. It's very easy to follow. I feel much better, too."*

Jeanie, Lincoln, Nebraska

# 15

# Entrées

While it isn't so in some European countries, in the United States an entrée is defined as the principle dish of the meal. I suggest that most days you keep your entrées simple, reserving dishes that require complex preparation (such as a rolled, stuffed roast) for special occasions. This is especially important when you are entertaining. After all, your guests are there to visit with you, not to have you in the kitchen all evening chopping, basting, baking, and sautéing.

As a general rule, we immediately think of beef, pork, lamb, chicken, turkey, and fish as choices for entrées. And this is fine because a moderate amount of meat prepared in a healthful way can be a part of a nutritious eating pattern. However, consider serving meatless entrées as well. I've included some great vegetarian recipes in this chapter. Try the Vegetable Lasagna, Stuffed Chiles, or—are you ready for this?—my No Flour, No Sugar Pizza.

## Cooking Meat

There may be nothing that pleases a meat eater more than a charbroiled steak, yet recent studies suggest that charring and heavy browning when frying and grilling meat may be damaging to your health.

The National Institutes of Health reports that cooking certain meats at temperatures so high that charring occurs creates chemicals that are not present in uncooked meats. A few of these chemicals may increase the risk of some kinds of cancer. For example, heterocyclic amines (HCAs) are the carcinogenic chemicals formed from the cooking of meats such as beef, pork, fowl, and fish. HCAs form when amino acids (the building blocks of proteins) and creatine (a chemical found in muscles) react at high cooking temperatures.

Interestingly enough, Michigan State University researchers report that adding cherries to ground beef patties before grilling reduces formation of some of these compounds thought to cause cancer. Cherry-spiked hamburgers? Don't laugh, schools in sixteen states now serve cherry beef burgers and they are said to be juicier and more tender than standard burgers.

What's the bottom line? As is true in all things, moderation is the key. It's okay to have a weekend barbecue now and then, but don't overdo it. And give that cherry thing a try.

## A Bit on Beef

Beef is packed full of essential nutrients such as protein, B vitamins, iron, and zinc. And it is extremely versatile if you consider that this is where we get burgers, steak, roasts, and much more. Be sure to choose lean cuts. Even hamburger is now available with only about 5 to 7 percent fat. Trim the fat off steaks and other cuts before cooking. Roast on racks so the fat drips away from the meat. The leaner the beef, the better it is for you.

## Lean Pork

Remember the ads that were running a number of years ago touting pork as the "other white meat"? These were developed because many lean pork cuts are similar in fat content to a skinless chicken breast.

Just like other red meats, pork provides many essential nutrients including iron, magnesium, phosphorous, potassium, niacin, and vitamin $B_{12}$.

You might consider complimenting pork with rosemary, the zest of an orange, and a tablespoon or two of orange juice added during the final five minutes of broiling. The meat will absorb the flavor, and your kitchen will smell heavenly. If you are preparing a roast, place it on a rack in the pan to prevent it from sitting in its own juices. The tenderloin is the leanest cut of pork. A three-ounce serving contains only 120 calories and 2.98 grams of total fat. Other lean cuts include boneless loin roast, boneless loin chops, and boneless ham (extra lean).

A two-ounce serving of Canadian-style bacon contains only 86 calories and 3.9 grams of fat and may be substituted for regular bacon in many recipes.

## Fresh Fish

Fish and other seafood can play an important part in your diet. They are high in protein and low in fat and provide a range of healthful benefits. Fish is an excellent source of omega-3 fish oil. Known to be a cholesterol-lowering agent, omega-3 has recently come under study as a mood enhancer and may have other benefits as well. White-flesh fish is lower in fat than any other source of animal protein. In addition, fish does not contain the omega-6 "bad" fats commonly found in red meat. Since fish is one of the most perishable of foods, note how it is kept. It stores best on a bed of ice. Fresh oysters, clams, and mussels must be alive when purchased and stored. For this reason, don't put them in a plastic bag where they can't breathe. When you are going to be doing quite a bit of shopping, select your fish just before going to the checkout counter and refrigerate it as soon as you get home.

Always rinse your fish before cooking. Then, a good rule of thumb is to broil it for ten minutes per inch of thickness. Thus, if you have a skinless cut one and a half inches thick, broil it for fifteen minutes—seven and a half minutes on each side. If it has skin, do not flip it during cooking. Broiling longer will dry the fish out and make it less flavorful. You want your fish to be moist and cooked to perfection. If you prefer baking, the cooking time may be longer. A way of preserving the moisture in fish that is baked is to cover it lightly with dry white wine. The wine adds to the flavor and you will be pleased with the results.

## Versatile Chicken

Chicken is another versatile food and for this reason is often a good choice for guests. It can be broiled, baked, stuffed, fried in olive oil, used in a casserole, and prepared scores of other ways. If you are short on preparation time, consider simply broiling your chicken pieces and basting them with your favorite combination of seasonings.

Chicken is lower in fat than most other meats. Over half of the fat is unsaturated, the type that helps lower cholesterol. Since much of the fat in chicken is in the skin, it is best to remove it before eating. This can be done with the same fat-lowering result before or after cooking, but if you leave the skin on while cooking, the meat will remain more moist. Chicken should be cooked thoroughly and not left pink.

Choose chicken recipes that call for baking, roasting, grilling, or poaching as opposed to deep-fat frying or panfrying. Of course, sautéing in olive oil is acceptable and encouraged.

## Making a Vegetarian Choice

Vegetarians used to be the last ones invited over for dinner. But, with the health benefits of eating a mainly plant-based diet coming to light, vegetarians are finally having their day in the sun.

Consider serving a vegetarian entrée at least a couple of nights a week. My meatless Vegetable Lasagna is a good choice. The pasta is replaced by zucchini or eggplant strips and the dish is completed with tomatoes, onions, mushrooms, spinach, and three kinds of cheeses. It makes a well-balanced, delicious main dish.

Simple is fine, too. Steamed or sautéed vegetables served over brown rice are attractive and colorful and present a variety of textures. They are a nice change from a heavier meal. Consider including onions, red peppers, bok choy, zucchini, yellow squash, fresh garlic, mushrooms, broccoli florets, and even slivered almonds. A touch of sesame oil added to olive oil when sautéing adds a nice aromatic nutty flavor.

Spices you might want to add to vegetarian dishes include red pepper flakes and fresh basil. A side salad with chopped walnuts and a sprinkling of freshly grated Parmesan cheese will produce attractive results, and the meal will please the vegetarian in each of us.

## Presentation

Nutritious foods are also tasty foods, but any food tastes better when it looks appetizing. Spend a little time planning how your food will look when you serve it. Take a hint from photos you see in magazines, or study how plates are served and garnished in expensive restaurants. Sometimes all it takes is a sprig of parsley or a lemon wedge to make all the difference.

Make it fun and enjoy your cooking!

# Asparagus and Chicken Pasta

*Patty Cox, Mooresville, North Carolina*

Pasta can be a part of your No Flour, No Sugar Diet. That is, if it is rice pasta made with whole rice and not rice flour. The vegetables in this dish combine to create a colorful, healthful, and flavor-rich meal.

One 1-pound bag rice pasta (made with whole rice, not rice flour)
1 cup shredded carrot
1 red bell pepper, seeded and sliced into strips
1 orange bell pepper, seeded and sliced into strips
1 medium red onion, diced
2 cloves garlic, minced
½ pound asparagus spears, cut into bite-size pieces
Cooking spray, for coating
1 pound skinless, boneless chicken breast, cubed
½ cup extra virgin olive oil
1 tablespoon dried basil
1 teaspoon dried oregano
Salt and black pepper to taste
One 7-ounce can corn
1 cup grape tomatoes, for garnish
½ cup chopped fresh parsley, for garnish

Cook pasta according to package instructions.

Place carrot, peppers, onion, garlic, and asparagus in large skillet coated with cooking spray. On medium heat, sauté about 5 minutes. Add chicken. Cook until meat is no longer pink and veggies are tender, 10 to 15 minutes.

In small bowl, combine oil, basil, oregano, salt, and pepper. Set aside.

Drain pasta and return to pot. Add in chicken mixture and corn. Mix well. Pour in oil mixture. Toss to coat. Garnish with tomatoes and parsley and serve.

*Serves 6 to 8*

# Vegetarian Pasta in a Skillet

*Glenn Miller, Canaan, Connecticut*

The crushed bouillon cube and slivered almonds make this colorful dish outstanding. If portobello mushrooms aren't available, substitute fresh brown mushrooms.

8 ounces whole rice pasta
1 cup sliced baby portobello mushrooms
¾ cup julienned roasted red bell peppers
3 cloves garlic, slivered
¾ cup broccoli florets
¾ cup sliced yellow squash
2 tablespoons butter
1 beef bouillon cube, crushed
¼ cup slivered almonds
2 tablespoons chopped fresh chives, for garnish

Cook pasta according to package directions.

Sauté mushrooms, red pepper, garlic, broccoli, and squash in large skillet in butter until tender, about 8 minutes. Drain cooked pasta and add to skillet. Sprinkle bouillion and almonds over mixture, stirring gently to combine. Heat through. Garnish with chives and serve.

*Serves 3 to 4*

# Pastaless Lasagna

*Jacqueline Ribes, Naples, Florida*

This low-carb dish will please nondieters who think a meal isn't a meal without carbs. It is wonderful when accompanied by a simple side salad of fresh field greens. When the tomato juice is simmering down, you can add onions, green peppers, or whatever you'd like.

1½ pounds lean ground beef
One 14-ounce can diced tomatoes with basil and garlic, with
   juice
Cooking spray, for coating
1 small jar of your favorite sugar-free spaghetti sauce
One 14-ounce can diced tomatoes with basil and garlic, well
   drained
2 eggs beaten with a splash of cream
One 15-ounce tub ricotta cheese
Salt and black pepper to taste
8 ounces shredded mozzarella cheese

Preheat oven to 350 degrees.

Brown ground beef in skillet; drain off excess juices. Add diced tomatoes with juice. Let simmer until all liquid is cooked down. This may take ½ hour or more on medium-high heat. Stir occasionally. It is important to totally reduce liquid, as lasagna will be runny and not properly set to cut if you don't.

Coat casserole with cooking spray. Place thin layer of meat mixture on bottom of casserole. Spread thin layer of spaghetti sauce over meat. Add drained diced tomatoes. In small bowl, combine eggs with ricotta, season with salt and pepper, and spread generous layer over tomatoes. Add another thin layer of meat mixture and repeat—sauce, tomatoes, ricotta. Finish with another thin layer of sauce and top generously with shredded mozzarella. Bake, uncovered, 45 minutes, or until browned and bubbling. Let cool 15 minutes before cutting and serving.

*Serves 6*

# Vegetarian Tacos

Be sure the taco shells are made with corn, not corn flour. This is a flavorful vegetarian version of tacos, and you'll find you don't miss the meat. The cabbage adds an unusual yet flavorful twist. You can also garnish the tacos with all your usual favorites—minced onion, chopped fresh tomatoes, salsa, and avocado slices.

Vegetable spray, for coating
½ medium onion, chopped
½ red bell pepper, chopped
1 small zucchini, shredded
1 cup pinto beans, drained and rinsed
8 crisp corn taco shells (made with corn, not corn flour)
½ cup grated cheddar cheese
1 cup shredded cabbage
Jalapeño rings, for garnish (optional)

Coat skillet with vegetable spray. Sauté onion and bell pepper over medium-high heat until soft but not browned, about 6 minutes. Add zucchini and cook until tender, about 5 minutes. Add pinto beans and heat until warm. Divide filling among taco shells. Sprinkle 1 tablespoon cheese and 2 tablespoons of cabbage on each taco. Garnish with jalapeño rings, if desired, and serve.

*Serves 4*

# Stir-fried Beef with Bean Threads

This dish is good served on cooked rice. The bean threads, made from ground mung beans, not flour, are flavorless but readily acquire the taste of the foods they accompany. Bean threads can be found in the Asian section of better supermarkets.

1 beef flank steak (about ¾ pound), fat trimmed
2 cloves garlic, minced
One 1-inch-long piece of fresh ginger, peeled and minced or
    grated
2 tablespoons sugar-free tamari sauce
2 tablespoons unsweetened apple juice
1 tablespoon cider vinegar
One 5-ounce package bean threads (*saifun*)
Boiling water, to cover bean threads
Cooking spray, for coating
1 red bell pepper, cut into strips
¼ pound fresh green beans, tips removed
1 cup peeled and thinly, diagonally sliced carrots
¼ cup chopped green onion
1 teaspoon Asian sesame oil

Wrap steak in waxed paper and lay flat in freezer about 15 minutes. (This makes it easier to cut thin.)

In medium bowl, while steak is chilling, mix together garlic, ginger, tamari sauce, apple juice, and cider vinegar.

Cut steak in half lengthwise on a cutting board, then into ½"-thick slices. Put slices into bowl of tamari mixture and let marinate at room temperature 30 minutes.

Prepare bean threads while beef is marinating by placing threads in large bowl and cover with boiling water. Let stand 20 or 30 minutes.

Drain. Put mass on cutting board and cut into quarters, to form 4 equal portions.

Coat large nonstick skillet with cooking spray. Heat over medium-high heat. Drain steak, reserving marinade. Add meat to skillet and stir-fry 1 or 2 minutes until lightly browned. Meat will be rare. Remove meat with slotted spoon to plate. If it's necessary, spray the skillet again with cooking spray. Sauté bell pepper, green beans, and carrots 3 or 4 minutes until vegetables are tender crisp. Add reserved marinade and cook, stirring often, 2 minutes to blend and heat thoroughly. Add meat, green onion, and sesame oil and cook 1 minute.

Place bean threads on 4 dinner plates or in pasta bowls. Divide meat mixture among plates and serve.

*Serves 4*

# Faux Spaghetti

Spaghetti squash has the look of spaghetti, hence its name. It will satisfy any pasta lover's craving. This dish looks and tastes just as delicious as traditional carb-heavy pasta.

1 spaghetti squash
1½ pounds lean ground beef
2 cloves garlic, minced
4 ounces fresh mushrooms, sliced
1 teaspoon butter
26 ounces sugar-free tomato sauce
1 cup grated Parmesan cheese
Water

Cut spaghetti squash in half, removing seeds. Place in microwave-safe dish with 1" water. Cover with plastic wrap and microwave on high until tender, about 15 minutes.

Over medium heat, brown meat, garlic, and mushrooms in butter, about 10 minutes. When they're fully cooked, add tomato sauce. Simmer a few minutes until thoroughly heated. With fork, shred squash into large bowl. (Its appearance will resemble spaghetti.) Divide among 4 plates and top with meat sauce. Sprinkle with cheese and serve.

*Serves 4*

# Tex-Mex Chili

This full-bodied dish can be made more robust by including the jalapeño seeds. It goes a long way and makes an excellent dish for a number of hungry individuals. It freezes well.

1 pound lean ground beef
1 pound linguisa or hot Italian sausage, chopped into bite-
   size pieces
1 medium yellow onion, chopped
1 red bell pepper, seeded and chopped
1 green bell pepper, seeded and chopped
One 15-ounce can dark red kidney beans, with liquid
One 15-ounce can diced tomatoes, with liquid
1 large jalapeño, seeded and chopped
1 teaspoon Splenda
Red pepper flakes to taste (optional)
Chili powder to taste

Brown beef and sausage in large pot over medium heat. Add onion and red and green peppers and cook until al dente, about 7 minutes. Stir in kidney beans, tomatoes, jalapeño, and Splenda and simmer about 10 minutes. Add red pepper flakes and chili powder (be sure to taste chili as you go to find desired heat level). Cook over medium-low heat until all veggies are tender and chili thickens, about 30 minutes. Serve.

*Serves 8 to 10*

# Crab Bake

This is an excellent low-carb alternative to crab cakes. Serve with a fresh green salad for a light meal.

1 egg, beaten
3 tablespoons sugar-free mayonnaise
2 teaspoons dry mustard
½ teaspoon salt
⅛ teaspoon black pepper
2 teaspoons celery seed
1 teaspoon dried parsley
¼ teaspoon Old Bay seasoning
1 pound fresh or canned lump crabmeat, shell pieces
    removed

Preheat oven to 350 degrees.

In medium bowl, combine egg, mayonnaise, mustard, salt, pepper, celery seed, parsley, and Old Bay seasoning. Set aside. Make sure there is no shell in crabmeat. Mix mayonnaise mixture and crabmeat together. Spoon into 4 small ovenproof containers and bake 20 to 25 minutes, or until tops are golden brown and bubbling. Serve hot.

*Serves 4*

# Oatmeal Meat Loaf

Ground turkey makes this low fat, and the oatmeal, in place of traditional bread crumbs, makes it low carb—leading to an all-around nutritious meal.

1½ pounds lean ground turkey
1 cup quick-cooking oats
½ cup egg substitute or 3 eggs
One 15-ounce can diced tomatoes with garlic and basil
1 package onion soup mix

Preheat oven to 325 degrees.

In large bowl, combine turkey, oats, egg substitute or eggs, ¾ can tomatoes, and soup mix until blended thoroughly. Place in 4" x 8" loaf pan and cover with remaining tomatoes. Bake until well done, about 1½ hours. Let stand 10 minutes before serving.

*Serves 6*

> *"I am having good luck without sugar or flour in my diet. Most of all, I don't miss it. In two months I have lost twenty-three pounds, I feel great, have more energy, and don't feel like I'm on a diet."*
>
> **Betty, Visalia, California**

# Red Wine Chops

The inclusion of red wine and cabbage in this recipe creates a distinctive flavor sure to please. This makes great wintertime fare.

2 medium yellow onions, chopped
2 cloves garlic, minced
4 tablespoons extra virgin olive oil
2 pounds boneless pork chops
1 pound cabbage, chopped
One 15-ounce can diced tomatoes, with liquid
Salt and black pepper to taste
1 cup dry red wine

In large skillet over medium-high heat, brown onions and garlic in oil. Add chops and sear until golden brown, about 3 minutes on each side. Place onion, garlic, and chops in large pot, layering on cabbage, tomatoes, and salt and pepper. Cover and simmer on low heat 30 minutes. Add wine and cook, covered, additional 5 to 10 minutes. Serve.

*Serves 4*

# Beanless Chili

This takeoff on a traditional chili dish is full flavored and perfect for group gatherings. Serve with corn bread for a heartier meal. Leftovers freeze well.

2 pounds lean ground beef
1 medium onion, chopped
2 cloves garlic, minced
One 15-ounce can diced tomatoes with chiles
One 15-ounce can diced tomatoes with basil and garlic
1 cup water
½ teaspoon ground oregano
½ teaspoon ground cumin
1 tablespoon cornstarch
3 tablespoons chili powder
2 tablespoons extra virgin olive oil
Salt and black pepper to taste

In large soup pot over medium-high heat, brown beef, onion, and garlic. Add remaining ingredients. Cover, reduce heat to medium low, and simmer 1 hour. Serve.

*Serves 6 to 8*

# Scallops on a Skewer

Break out of the mundane and add a touch of class to your evening meal with this attractive presentation. Complete the meal with brown rice and a fresh green salad. If using wooden skewers, be sure to soak them in water first, so they won't catch fire.

½ teaspoon minced garlic
¼ teaspoon paprika
2 tablespoons orange juice
8 large sea scallops
1 medium zucchini
Cooking spray, for coating

Combine garlic, paprika, and orange juice in small bowl. Add scallops and marinate 30 minutes in refrigerator.

Light outdoor grill or preheat broiler.

Cut zucchini into thin strips lengthwise, discarding ends. Remove scallops from bowl, reserving marinade. Roll zucchini strips around each scallop and secure with skewer, placing 4 scallops on each skewer.

Coat grill rack with cooking spray before placing scallops on, or use small baking sheet covered with aluminum foil and cooking spray before broiling. Cook each side 4 minutes, or until done. Baste with reserved marinade during cooking. Serve.

*Serves 2*

# Stuffed Peppers

Create a festive look by using red, yellow, or orange peppers. This dish is very good with stuffed baked potatoes and a tossed green salad.

½ pound turkey sausage
1 cup cooked rice
1 egg, beaten
1 cup fresh, canned, or frozen corn
1 teaspoon salt
¼ teaspoon black pepper
2 large bell peppers, stemmed, seeded, and cut top to
    bottom

Preheat oven to 350 degrees.

Mix sausage, rice, egg, corn, salt, and pepper in medium bowl. Put ¼ mixture in each pepper half. Bake 30 minutes, or until internal temperature reads 165 degrees on meat thermometer. Serve.

*Serves 4*

# Swordfish Kabobs

This colorful dish can be prepared on a grill or broiled indoors. It blends spicy and sweet to make a great meal. Serve with brown rice.

¼ cup rice wine vinegar
1 tablespoon lime juice
½ teaspoon lime zest
¼ teaspoon chili powder
¼ teaspoon cayenne pepper
¼ teaspoon crushed red pepper flakes
1 pound swordfish steaks, cut into cubes
1 fresh pineapple, peeled and cubed, or one 20-ounce can
    sugar-free pineapple chunks
1 medium green bell pepper, stemmed, seeded, and cut into
    1" slices
½ pound grape tomatoes
Cooking spray, for coating

If using wooden skewers, submerge them in water and let stand until soaked.

Combine vinegar, lime juice and zest, chili powder, cayenne, and red pepper flakes in large bowl. Add swordfish chunks, pineapple, pepper, and tomatoes. Marinate in refrigerator 1 hour.

Light outdoor grill or preheat broiler.

Coat grill rack or baking sheet with cooking spray. Remove ingredients from bowl, reserving the liquid. On 8 metal or soaked wooden skewers, alternate swordfish, pineapple, pepper, and tomatoes. Grill over medium heat or broil about 5 minutes per side until fully cooked. Additional marinade may be used to baste during cooking. Serve.

*Serves 4*

# Jasmine Turkey Rice

This quick and easy dish is a great summertime meal. Serve with a side salad.

1 pound lean ground turkey
Cooking spray, for coating
1½ cups water
½ teaspoon salt
One 15-ounce can diced tomatoes with chiles
1 cup uncooked jasmine rice
One 7-ounce can corn

Brown turkey in pan coated with cooking spray. Drain and add water, salt, tomatoes, and rice. Cover and simmer 10 to 15 minutes over low heat, or until rice is tender and all liquid is absorbed. Stir in corn and heat through before serving.

*Serves 4*

# Dijon-Crusted Tilapia

Tilapia has become a very popular fish. It's widely farmed and quickly cooked. It's got a mild, sweet taste and works well in many recipes calling for fish fillets.

½ cup finely chopped pecans
4 teaspoons sugar-free Dijon-style mustard
4 tilapia or other firm white fish fillets
Cooking spray, for coating

Preheat oven to 350 degrees.

Toast pecans in dry pan over medium heat, stirring frequently, being careful not to burn them. This will take only a few minutes. Remove from heat and place on plate. Spread mustard over 1 side of each fillet. Dredge each, mustard side down, in pecans.

Coat baking sheet with cooking spray. Place fillets, mustard side up, on sheet. Bake about 5 minutes, or until fish flakes. Serve.

*Serves 4*

# Vegetable Loaf

This dish goes well with asparagus spears and spicy baked apples.

8 ounces silken tofu, drained
1 pound lean ground turkey
1 egg, beaten
1 cup nonfat milk
½ tablespoon dried parsley
½ tablespoon dried basil
1 teaspoon salt
½ teaspoon black pepper
1 cup instant mashed potato flakes
1 cup frozen peas
1 cup shredded cabbage
1 medium potato, thinly sliced
1 large carrot, thinly sliced
1 celery stalk, diced
1 medium onion, finely diced
Cooking spray, for coating
½ cup grated cheese of your choice

Preheat oven to 350 degrees.

In large bowl, combine tofu and ground turkey, mixing well. Next add egg, milk, seasonings, and potato flakes. Mix in vegetables. Place in large casserole dish coated with cooking spray. Cover and bake 55 to 60 minutes. Add cheese to top in last 5 minutes of cooking so it becomes bubbly. Serve hot.

*Serves 4 to 6*

# Chicken "Paella"

This is a simple takeoff on Spanish-style paella. It is a one-dish meal with a little bit of everything, sure to win over your taste buds. Linguisa is a Portuguese smoked garlic sausage with a unique and delightful flavor.

1 pound skinless, boneless chicken breasts
1 cup lemon juice
1 teaspoon paprika
2 teaspoons extra virgin olive oil
1 large onion, coarsely chopped
1 red bell pepper, stemmed, seeded, and coarsely chopped
3 cloves garlic, minced
One 7-ounce can peas or 4 to 6 ounces fresh snow peas
6 ounces linguisa, chunked
One 28-ounce can diced tomatoes
1 pound medium shrimp, uncooked
One 7-ounce can whole black olives, drained
3 cups hot cooked rice
¼ cup chopped fresh parsley, for garnish

In large skillet, marinate chicken breasts in lemon juice and paprika in refrigerator 1 hour.

In deep saucepan, over medium-high heat, combine oil, onion, bell pepper, garlic, and peas. Sauté until tender, about 3 minutes. Add linguisa and cook additional 3 minutes. Add tomatoes and stir well. Reduce heat and simmer while cooking chicken.

Bring chicken breasts to a boil in lemon juice in skillet. Reduce heat and simmer until chicken is fully cooked, about 15 minutes. Remove from heat and cut into bite-size pieces. Combine linguisa mixture with chicken. Stir in shrimp and cook until shrimp are just pink, about 3 minutes. Do not overcook or they will be chewy. Stir in black olives just before serving. Serve over rice and sprinkle with parsley.

*Serves 4 to 6*

# Green Onion Steak

The full flavor of fresh ginger is the key to success in this recipe.

1 pound steak, fat trimmed
¼ cup sugar-free tamari sauce
1 clove garlic, minced
½ teaspoon peeled and grated fresh ginger
¼ cup extra virgin olive oil
1 large red bell pepper, cut into ½-inch strips
2 celery stalks, chopped
1 cup diagonally sliced green onions
1 tablespoon cornstarch
1 cup water
2 large plum tomatoes, quartered

Cut steak into ⅛"-thick strips. Combine with tamari, garlic, and ginger in medium bowl. Mix and set aside while preparing vegetables.

In large pan, heat oil over medium-high heat and stir in beef mixture. Cook until browned, stirring frequently. Add in red pepper, celery, and green onion and cook until al dente, about 5 minutes. Mix cornstarch with water and add to pan, stirring constantly, until thickened. Add tomatoes and heat through. Serve.

*Serves 4*

# Tarragon Thyme Chicken

This is an excellent, mild alternative to the usual chicken with rosemary. Serve with a baked stuffed tomato and side salad.

Cooking spray, for coating
3 whole skinless, boneless chicken breasts, halved
½ tablespoon dried tarragon
½ tablespoon dried thyme
1 teaspoon salt
1 teaspoon black pepper
1 teaspoon dried basil
2 cloves garlic, minced
1 large lemon, sliced

Preheat oven to 350 degrees.

Coat 9" x 13" baking dish with cooking spray. Place in chicken. In small bowl, mix all seasonings and garlic together and sprinkle over chicken breasts. Top with lemon slices. Bake 40 minutes, or until done. Serve.

*Serves 6*

# Vegetable Lasagna

Zucchini slices form the basis for this one-dish meal, a healthful and delicious alternative to traditional lasagna. It is filling and nutritious and won't expand your waistline.

One 15-ounce can diced tomatoes, drained
1 medium onion, chopped
2 cloves garlic, minced
¼ teaspoon dried basil
¼ teaspoon salt
½ teaspoon black pepper
¼ teaspoon dried oregano
12 ounces ricotta cheese
1½ cups shredded mozzarella cheese
1 teaspoon dried parsley
3 medium zucchini (about 9" long)
1½ cups sliced fresh mushrooms
One 10-ounce package frozen chopped spinach, thawed and
    squeezed dry
2 tablespoons grated Parmesan cheese

Preheat oven to 350 degrees.

Combine tomatoes, onion, garlic, basil, salt, pepper, and oregano in small bowl and set aside, reserving ½ cup for top layer. In separate bowl, combine ricotta, mozzarella, and parsley. Set aside. Cut off both ends of zucchini and slice lengthwise into strips. Arrange strips in 8" x 8" baking dish to cover bottom of dish. Spread ½ of ricotta mixture over zucchini. Next layer ½ of tomato sauce mixture, then ½ of mushrooms, followed by ½ of spinach. Repeat with zucchini, ricotta, sauce, mushrooms, and spinach. Top with reserved ½ cup sauce and Parmesan. Bake 30 to 45 minutes. Serve.

*Serves 4 to 6*

# Stuffed Chiles

The smoky flavor of cumin brings out the spicy Southwest essence of this dish.

6 medium poblano chiles
One 15-ounce can black beans, drained
1½ cups low-fat shredded taco-blend cheese
1 medium onion, chopped
1 cup egg substitute
1½ cups nonfat milk
¼ teaspoon ground cumin
¼ teaspoon dried oregano
⅛ teaspoon cayenne pepper
2 cloves garlic, minced
1 jar sugar-free salsa

Preheat oven to 350 degrees.

Roast chiles under broiler until blistered on both sides. Place in plastic bag 5 to 10 minutes. Peel skin off. Slice open one side and remove seeds and stems. Place flat in casserole dish. Layer beans over chiles with 1¼ cups cheese and onion. Fold chiles in half in dish. Mix egg substitute with milk, cumin, oregano, cayenne, and garlic. Pour over chiles. Top with remaining cheese. Bake until set, 30 to 40 minutes. Serve with salsa.

*Serves 6*

# Sausage-Stuffed Apples

These stuffed apples are very good served with curried rice.

4 large apples
1 teaspoon ground cinnamon
4 dashes of salt
½ pound turkey sausage

Preheat oven to 375 degrees.

Cut slice from tops of apples. Scoop out and discard cores, leaving bottoms of apples intact. Scoop out apple pulp and reserve, leaving shells about ½" thick. Sprinkle inside of each apple with cinnamon and dash of salt. Chop apple pulp and mix with sausage. Stuff mixture into apple shells. Place stuffed apples in baking dish and bake 20 to 30 minutes until apples are tender and sausage is cooked. Serve.

*Serves 4*

> *"My husband and I have been quite satisfied with what we consider to be our new way of living with food. My husband has lost forty pounds and I have lost twenty-five to date, with more to come, I am certain."*
>
> **Mary Ann, Naples, Florida**

# No Flour, No Sugar Pizza

The secret to this pizza is the rice crust. Everyone in the family will love it. Great for munching while watching a football game on TV.

### Crust

3 cups cold cooked rice

2 eggs, beaten

1 cup shredded mozzarella cheese

Cooking spray, for coating

### Sauce

2 cloves garlic, minced

One 15-ounce can diced tomatoes, with juice

½ teaspoon dried basil

½ teaspoon dried oregano

### Suggested Toppings

1 cup grated mozzarella cheese

1 cup diced grilled chicken

1 cup of your favorite vegetables (mushrooms, black olives,
    bell peppers, onions, broccoli, spinach, tomatoes)

Preheat oven to 450 degrees.

In medium bowl, mix together rice, eggs, and mozzarella until well combined. Coat 12" or 13" pizza pan with cooking spray. Pat crust mixture firmly into pan. Bake 20 minutes, or until lightly browned.

Coat skillet with cooking spray. Sauté garlic over medium-high heat 1 or 2 minutes. Do not brown. Add tomatoes with juice and herbs. Bring to a boil, then reduce heat and simmer 10 minutes, or until thickened.

Spread sauce over baked crust. Sprinkle cheese over, then add toppings. Bake another 10 minutes, or until cheese is melted. Serve hot.

*Serves 4*

# Ratatouille on Squash

This is a delicious way to fill your daily veggie requirement.

1 medium eggplant, cubed
1 red bell pepper, stemmed, seeded, and sliced
1 onion, sliced
2 cloves garlic, minced
2 tablespoons extra virgin olive oil
1 medium yellow squash, sliced
1 medium zucchini, sliced
8 ounces mushrooms, sliced
2 large tomatoes, sliced
1 teaspoon dried basil
1 teaspoon dried oregano
½ teaspoon salt
½ teaspoon black pepper
1 large spaghetti squash (about 2 pounds)
1 cup shredded mozzarella cheese

In large skillet over medium-high heat, sauté eggplant, red pepper, onion, and garlic in oil 5 minutes. Add yellow squash, zucchini, mushrooms, and tomatoes. Simmer, covered, stirring occasionally, until tender. Uncover, add spices, and simmer 5 additional minutes. Cut spaghetti squash in half and remove seeds. Place in microwave-safe dish with 1" water and cover with plastic wrap. Cook on high about 15 minutes until soft. Remove squash strands with fork and place on platters. Spoon ratatouille over top, sprinkle with shredded cheese, and serve.

*Serves 4*

# Saffron Chicken

Saffron, a delicious spice, adds a unique flavor and color to this dish. It works well for special-occasion meals.

6 skinless, boneless chicken breasts, rinsed and patted dry
1 teaspoon salt
1 teaspoon paprika
½ cup extra virgin olive oil
3 tablespoons butter
¼ teaspoon saffron
1 cup uncooked rice
2 bay leaves
½ cup pimentos, chopped
One 12-ounce package frozen peas
½ cup sliced black olives
1 cup 99 percent fat-free chicken broth

Preheat oven to 350 degrees.

Season chicken with salt and paprika. Place in large skillet over medium heat and slowly brown in oil and butter 10 minutes, turning occasionally. Stir in saffron and rice. Place bay leaves in bottom of 9" x 13" baking dish. Add the rice, chicken, pimentos, peas, olives, and broth. Cover and bake 1 hour, or until tender. Add water if necessary during cooking. Serve.

*Serves 6 to 8*

# Pork Sausage Patties

Serve with peppers and onions for a flavorful meal. A side salad is another perfect complement.

1 pound lean ground pork
1 egg, beaten
2 tablespoons water
¼ teaspoon pepper
¼ teaspoon dried sage
⅛ teaspoon ground allspice
⅛ teaspoon dried dill
⅛ teaspoon hot sauce
¼ teaspoon dried basil
¼ teaspoon dried oregano
⅛ teaspoon chili powder
⅛ teaspoon garlic powder

Preheat broiler.

Mix all ingredients thoroughly. Shape into 4 patties about ½" thick and place on a rack in a shallow pan. Broil 6 inches from the heat until well done, turning halfway through cooking. Serve.

*Serves 4*

# Tuscany Duck with Blueberry Glaze

This recipe takes a little more time, but don't let that frighten you. Duck breast is dark and rich, similar to beef, and well worth the little bit of extra effort. Use one duck breast and cut the rest of the ingredients in half if you want to make this a romantic dinner for two.

2 Muscovy duck breasts (magret)
Salt and black pepper to taste
¼ cup dried blueberries
½ cup red wine
Cooking spray, for coating
2 shallots, finely minced
2 cloves garlic, finely minced
4 cups fresh baby spinach
One 15-ounce can cannellini beans, drained and rinsed
1 tablespoon extra virgin olive oil
2 tablespoons pine nuts, for garnish
2 tablespoons finely minced red bell pepper, for garnish
2 tablespoons minced fresh parsley, for garnish

Score fat on both duck breasts. Season with salt and pepper. Soak blueberries in wine. Set aside.

Sear each side of duck breast 1 minute in skillet over medium-high heat, then cook, fat side down, 7 to 10 minutes, or until fat is golden. Turn over and cook another 3 to 5 minutes on medium heat until medium rare. Remove from heat and keep warm. Deglaze pan with wine-soaked blueberries. Cook 1 or 2 minutes until slightly thickened.

Coat another skillet with cooking spray. Sauté shallots and garlic over medium-high heat about 1 minute. Add spinach and cook until wilted. Season with salt and pepper. Add beans and cook 3 to 4 minutes until heated through.

Spoon spinach and bean mixture onto platter. Slice duck breasts and place on top. Pour blueberry-wine sauce over. Drizzle with olive oil, garnish with pine nuts, red pepper, and parsley, and serve.

*Serves 4*

# Hedgehog Meatballs

Spikes of rice make this a fun food to serve kids and adults alike. Serve with a fresh green salad and Pureed Cauliflower (see page 214).

2 pounds lean ground beef
1½ cups uncooked brown rice
2 eggs, beaten
½ teaspoon salt
1 teaspoon black pepper
1 teaspoon onion powder
1 teaspoon garlic powder
1 medium head cabbage, coarsely chopped
1 medium onion, chopped
1 green bell pepper, stemmed, seeded, and chopped
1 cup sugar-free tomato sauce
1 cup water
1 beef bouillon cube

Mix beef, rice, eggs, salt, pepper, and onion and garlic powders together to form meatballs. Layer cabbage, onion, and green pepper in bottom of slow cooker or Crock-Pot. Add meatballs on top. Pour sauce and water in along with bouillon cube. Cook on low about 7 hours. Serve.

*Serves 4 to 6*

# Fall Harvest Casserole

This recipe is based on English pork pie. The traditional chunks of pork roast have been replaced with ground pork to make it a faster meal. You can find lean ground pork in the stores these days, but still be sure to drain it well after browning. The traditional pastry crust is replaced with a sweet potato topping.

1 pound lean ground pork
½ medium onion, diced
1 teaspoon dried sage
½ teaspoon dried thyme
½ teaspoon dried oregano
¼ teaspoon ground coriander
1 teaspoon salt
½ teaspoon black pepper
1 medium apple, diced
¼ cup sugar-free apple juice

**Topping**

2 medium sweet potatoes
1 tablespoon butter
⅛ teaspoon ground nutmeg
½ teaspoon salt
½ cup evaporated skim milk (more or less, as needed)
Cooking spray, for coating

Preheat oven to 350 degrees.

In skillet, brown and crumble pork over medium-high heat. Drain off fat. Add onion and sauté 4 to 5 minutes until onion is soft. Add herbs and spices and stir to combine. Add apple and apple juice, reduce heat, and simmer 5 minutes.

Pierce sweet potatoes to vent and microwave on high about 8 minutes, or until soft. Cut in half, remove pulp, and mash in medium bowl with butter, nutmeg, salt, and milk, adding just enough milk to make thick but creamy sweet potato mash.

Coat 2-quart round baking dish with cooking spray. Spoon filling into dish and top with sweet potatoes. Coat potatoes with cooking spray. Bake 30 to 45 minutes. Serve.

*Serves 4*

# Chicken Pot Pie

Everyone loves a homemade chicken pot pie. In this version, hash browned potatoes create a delicious crust.

2 skinless, boneless chicken breasts, cooked and chopped
One 10-ounce can 98 percent fat-free cream of mushroom
    soup
One 7-ounce can sliced carrots, well drained
½ cup sliced mushrooms
One 7-ounce can peas, drained
¾ cup water
4 frozen hash brown patties

Preheat oven to 375 degrees.

Place all ingredients except hash brown patties in 6" x 9" baking dish. Cover with patties. Bake, uncovered, 45 to 55 minutes. Serve hot.

*Serves 3 to 4*

## 16

## *Side Dishes*

**M**an does not live by bread alone. Nor do we live by single-dish meals alone—most of the time at least. Side dishes add a welcome variety to our meals, and when they are nutritious, good-tasting foods, all the better.

Side dishes may be selected for flavor, texture, or color to blend or contrast with other foods you are serving. If the main dish you are preparing is spicy, you might decide to serve a mild side dish as an offset or perhaps you'll choose something hearty that will stand up to spicy. Similarly, a lightly seasoned fish entrée could be complemented by mashed winter squash flavored with nutmeg. A better choice, however, might be something with a more delicate flavor that complements the fish's subtle seasoning. The possibilities are limitless, and it is often here, alongside the entrée, that one's true creativity and style can rise to the top.

### Give It Some Thought

Initially you should decide what results you want to achieve, or, to put it another way, what statement you want to make when your meal is served. Colorful, ample, simple, elegant, all of the above? Let's consider a few examples. If you are broiling chops, you might decide to serve baked sweet potatoes and lightly steamed green beans. Thus, you have an autumn orange and a bright green to complement the rich browns of the chops. You are offering a nice range of textures too, with the almost creamy-smooth texture of the potatoes and the crispness of the beans cooked al dente pairing well with the broiled meat.

Sides don't even have to go on the side. For a broiled steak, sauté a sliced medium-size onion in a tablespoon of olive oil. When the steak is almost done, spoon the onion over the top of the steak and pop it back under the broiler for a minute or two. This will enhance the flavor and the presentation of the steak. Additional sides you can include with this might be fresh corn on the cob in the summertime or steamed fresh asparagus in the spring. Boiled red potatoes with the skins left on would work well to round out this meal in any season. If you prefer, eliminate the potatoes and consider stuffed mushrooms—see chapter 11, on appetizers, for great, healthful recipes. Either way, your meal will be colorful, well balanced, and nourishing. Time, it seems, is in short supply to most of us these days. So, in addition to the recipes I've included in this chapter (which don't take long to make), here are a few very quick, nutritious no flour, no sugar dishes you can consider when selecting sides.

### Quinoa

Pronounced *'keen-wah*, this grain is an important staple in South American cuisine and is increasing in popularity in the United States. It is available packaged and is prepared similarly to rice. For a little more flavor, substitute fat-free chicken broth for water.

### Barley

Barley has a delightful, nutty flavor. As with quinoa, you can substitute fat-free chicken broth for more flavor. If you're really adventurous, try chamomile or jasmine tea instead of water or chicken broth when preparing it. Use about one tablespoon of steeped leaves to every cup of water recommended in a recipe. Tea has a way of turning this simple dish into an elegant one, which will delight your family and guests. To save more time, precook your barley and refrigerate or freeze it, then simply slip it into the microwave in a covered dish for a few minutes when you are ready to eat.

## Acorn Squash

Cut an acorn squash in half and place it, open side down, in a microwave-safe pan filled with ½" water. Cook on high 5 to 8 minutes, or until the squash is soft when pierced with a fork. Before serving, add a little butter, salt, and pepper or even an individual packet of Splenda for a sweet taste.

## Roasted or Grilled Broccoli

Place broccoli spears in a plastic food storage bag and pour in a couple of tablespoons of olive oil. Add salt and pepper and shake the bag, coating the broccoli evenly. Remove from the bag and put it in a covered pan. Roast at 350 degrees for about 20 minutes, removing the cover for the last few minutes. Or if you happen to be barbecuing or using a gas grill, place the broccoli on the grill over high heat. Turn once. Dare to allow the broccoli to blacken a little before removing it.

## Oven-baked Potato

A potato baked in a conventional oven will take almost an hour. While the skins will come out deliciously crusty, a similar effect can be accomplished in far less time. Start your potatoes in a microwave oven on high, heating 6 to 10 minutes, depending on size and number, until completely cooked. Transfer the potatoes to a conventional oven preheated to 400 degrees for about 5 minutes to crisp up the skins. You will have saved about 45 minutes.

## Steamed Vegetables

Most vegetables come out very well when steamed. With steaming you preserve most of the vegetables' nutrients that would otherwise be lost when they are boiled or sautéed. Further, the color of the vegetables will be greatly enhanced. If you don't have a steamer, you can purchase one at your local grocery store. They are inexpensive and made to fit into several sizes of saucepans. Simply put an inch or so of water in the bottom of your pan, place your vegetables on the steamer, cover the pan, and cook over medium-high heat. Your vegetables will steam to perfection in less than 5 minutes.

As you've likely heard me say before, healthful foods are tasty, but it helps to make your no flour, no sugar side dishes attractive and appetizing. So think about the bowls and plates you serve them in and on and the possible ways you can garnish them.

# Hot Sweet Corn Bread

*Dorothy Isaacs, Anadarko, Oklahoma*

This version provides a bit of Southwestern flavor and livens up any dish.

1 cup quick-cooking oatmeal
2 cups cornmeal
3 eggs
2 cups milk
⅓ cup extra virgin olive oil
1 medium onion, chopped
1 medium hot green pepper, finely chopped
¼ cup SugarTwin
4 teaspoons baking powder
1 teaspoon salt
Cooking spray, for coating

Preheat oven to 375 degrees.

Mix all ingredients in large bowl. Pour into 4" x 8" loaf pan coated with cooking spray. Bake 25 to 30 minutes, or until golden brown. Serve hot.

*Serves 8*

*"I am five foot one and weighed 234 pounds when I started Dr. Gott's No Flour, No Sugar Diet. I've been on it for four months and have lost 45 pounds. I tried every diet and diet pill known without any success. Thank you so much for improving my quality of life."*

*Marilyn, Princeton, New Jersey*

# Corn and Peppers

*Amy Campbell, Lancaster, Pennsylvania*

The bacon in this recipe provides a unique flavor. This is an absolute must-try.

3 ears fresh corn, cut and scraped
½ red onion, thinly sliced
2 red bell peppers, diced
2 green bell peppers, diced
2 yellow bell peppers, diced
6 slices bacon, cooked and chopped
One 12-ounce can 99 percent fat-free chicken broth
1 tablespoon white wine vinegar
¾ tablespoon julienned fresh sage

In medium saucepan, cook all ingredients over medium-high heat about 10 minutes. Serve warm.

*Serves 12*

# Southwestern Succotash

This is a delicious addition to most meals and can easily be doubled or tripled for dinner parties.

Cooking spray, for coating
1 clove garlic, minced
One 4-ounce can mild green chiles, chopped
1 green onion, chopped
2 medium zucchini, chopped
1 cup fresh or thawed frozen corn
¼ cup evaporated skim milk
¼ cup grated Monterey Jack cheese

Coat skillet with cooking spray. Over medium-high heat, cook garlic briefly, about 1 minute. Add chiles, green onion, zucchini, and corn, cooking about 5 minutes longer. Add milk and heat throughly. Stir in cheese and remove from heat. Continue stirring until cheese is melted. Serve warm.

*Serves 4*

# Cranberry Salad

Tired of vegetable sides every night? Why not try this delicious fruit side. The tart cranberries are great with a mild pork entrée.

1 package fresh cranberries
Juice of 1 medium orange
Zest of ½ medium orange
¾ cup Splenda
Two 0.3-ounce packages sugar-free raspberry Jell-O
2½ cups hot water
2 celery stalks, finely chopped
½ cup chopped walnuts
1 medium apple, cored, peeled, and chopped

Puree cranberries, orange juice and zest, and Splenda in food processor. Dissolve Jell-O in water. Add celery, walnuts, apple, and cranberry mixture to the Jell-O. Combine all ingredients in bowl and refrigerate until ready to serve.

*Serves 6*

# Sweet-and-Sour Cucumbers

For a more attractive presentation before slicing the cucumber, using a fork, scrape lines through the skin down the length of the cucumber all the way around. This will create an attractive flower-like appearance. The vinegar and Splenda make this recipe both sweet and sour.

2 cups sliced cucumbers
1 cup thinly sliced onion
¼ cup vinegar
¼ teaspoon salt

¼ teaspoon black pepper

¼ teaspoon dried dill

1 tablespoon Splenda

Wash cucumbers. Do not peel. Slice into ⅛" pieces from end to end, discarding both end pieces. Place in medium bowl. Add onion slices.

In separate small bowl, combine vinegar, salt, pepper, dill, and Splenda. Pour over cucumbers and onion. Chill 1 hour, tossing occasionally, before serving.

*Serves 6*

# Three-Bean Salad

This protein-rich dish is an excellent addition to any summertime meal and is a hit at parties or picnics.

One 14-ounce can cut green beans, drained

One 14-ounce can kidney beans, drained

One 14-ounce can chickpeas, drained

1 medium red onion, chopped

½ cup vinegar

¼ cup extra virgin olive oil

¼ cup Splenda

¼ teaspoon salt

¼ teaspoon black pepper

Place beans and chickpeas in medium bowl with chopped onion.

In separate small bowl, combine vinegar, oil, Splenda, salt, and pepper. Pour over veggies. Refrigerate 1 hour before serving.

*Serves 10 to 12*

# Black Bean Salad

For an attractive presentation, place this colorful salad on a bed of lettuce leaves.

One 19-ounce can black beans, drained
One 7-ounce can whole kernel corn, drained
One 7-ounce can chickpeas, drained
½ medium red onion, chopped
1 medium red bell pepper, chopped
3 tablespoons sugar-free Italian salad dressing
8 to 12 lettuce leaves

Blend all ingredients except lettuce leaves in bowl. Refrigerate. When ready to serve, place salad on lettuce leaves.

*Serves 8 to 12*

# Pureed Cauliflower

This is an excellent alternative to mashed potatoes and can be prepared in advance of dinner. Simply reheat it in the oven or microwave before serving.

1 head cauliflower, chopped (use florets only)
3 cloves garlic, chopped
One 14-ounce can 99 percent fat-free chicken broth
½ teaspoon salt
2 teaspoons butter
¼ cup grated Parmesan cheese
Fresh chives, for garnish

Combine cauliflower, garlic, broth, and salt in saucepan. Cover and simmer until extremely tender, about 10 minutes. Drain, reserving broth. Place cauliflower in food processor with butter. Puree, slowly adding broth as needed for mashed potato consistency. Gently stir in cheese before serving. Serve garnished with chives.

*Serves 4*

# Ratatouille

A traditional side with loads of flavor. For a twist, try using different varieties of eggplant such as the small Japanese eggplants.

4 medium-size zucchini, chopped
4 medium-size yellow squashes, chopped
1 large eggplant, chopped
One 15-ounce can diced tomatoes with basil and garlic, with
    liquid
1 cup chopped green onion
1 cup grated Parmesan cheese

Preheat oven to 325 degrees.

Place all ingredients except cheese in 8" x 8" baking dish. Cover with cheese. Bake 1 hour, or until vegetables are soft. Serve.

*Serves 4 to 6*

# Sweet Potato Bake

These sweet potatoes have a touch of spice that make this a great fall dish.

4 large sweet potatoes
One 20-ounce can sugar-free crushed pineapple
¼ teaspoon ground nutmeg
¼ teaspoon ground cinnamon
¼ teaspoon ground ginger
¼ teaspoon ground allspice

Preheat oven to 350 degrees.

Scrub potatoes and vent with fork. Cook in microwave 6 to 8 minutes, or until tender. Remove and slice in half lengthwise. Place pulp in bowl, retaining skins. Drain pineapple, reserving ½ of juice. Mash potatoes, spices, pineapple, and reserved juice. Fill potato skins with mixture and bake about 15 minutes, or until heated thoroughly. Serve warm.

*Serves 4 to 8*

# French-fried Sweet Potatoes

For French-fried potato lovers, this is a colorful complement to any meal.

Cooking spray, for coating
2 medium sweet potatoes, peeled and cut into ¼" strips
1 tablespoon extra virgin olive oil
Salt and black pepper to taste
1 teaspoon ground cinnamon
2 tablespoons Splenda

Preheat oven to 450 degrees.

Coat baking sheet with cooking spray. Place potatoes on baking sheet. Toss with oil, salt, and pepper. Bake, turning occasionally, 20 to 25 minutes, or until tender. Remove from oven. Sprinkle with cinnamon and Splenda. Serve.

*Serves 2*

# Veggie Barley

The flavor of barley is greatly enhanced when you use chicken broth in place of water. The vegetables in this dish provide additional depth of flavor. You can store any leftovers in the refrigerator in a tightly closed container for up to two weeks.

16 ounces uncooked barley
8 cups 99 percent fat-free chicken broth
3 tablespoons butter
8 ounces fresh mushrooms, sliced
2 medium onions, slivered
2 medium carrots, chopped
One 7-ounce can corn niblets

Combine barley, broth, butter, and veggies in Crock-Pot or slow cooker. Mix well. Cook on high 5 to 6 hours, stirring every 1 to 2 hours to ensure even cooking. This can also be done in the microwave or on stovetop. Follow barley package directions and cook until all liquid is absorbed. Serve.

*Serves 14*

# Tofu-Parmesan-Stuffed Mushrooms

This dish can be prepared in advance and simply popped into your oven about a half hour before you're ready to eat. It is an excellent side that will delight your guests.

8 ounces fresh button mushrooms
Cooking spray, for coating
½ small onion, chopped
2 cloves garlic, minced
8 ounces silken tofu, drained
½ cup grated Parmesan cheese

Preheat oven to 350 degrees.

Wash mushrooms, removing and reserving stems. Coat frying pan with cooking spray. Over medium-high heat, sauté finely chopped stems with onion and garlic about 5 minutes. Cool. Add tofu and ½ of cheese. Mix well. Fill mushroom caps with stem-tofu-cheese mixture. Place in greased baking dish and top with remaining cheese. Bake 25 to 30 minutes. Serve.

*Serves 6*

# Eggplant Casserole

This dish is full of color and flavor. It goes well with broiled lean hamburger patties.

¾ cup chopped onion
3 cloves garlic, chopped
⅓ cup extra virgin olive oil
4 red bell peppers, julienned
2½ cups sliced zucchini
2½ cups peeled and diced eggplant
One 15-ounce can chopped tomatoes, with liquid
2 teaspoons chopped fresh basil
Salt and black pepper to taste

Preheat oven to 350 degrees.

In large ovenproof skillet, sauté onion and garlic in olive oil over medium heat until tender. Add peppers, zucchini, eggplant, tomatoes, and basil. Bake in skillet 30 minutes, uncovered, to reduce liquid. Cover and bake 15 minutes longer.

Or, cook over medium heat on stovetop for same amount of time. Salt and pepper to taste and serve.

*Serves 8*

# Onion Mashed Potatoes

For a different take on mashed potatoes, try this recipe flavored with chicken bouillon and onion. You'll be pleasantly surprised. Because of the subtle chicken flavor in the potatoes, consider serving chicken as your entrée.

4 medium boiling potatoes, peeled and diced
Water to cover potatoes
2 chicken bouillon cubes
½ small onion, finely chopped
1 teaspoon onion powder

Place potatoes in large pot and cover with water. Bring to a boil and cook 15 minutes, or until soft. Drain, reserving 1⅓ cups of liquid. In small saucepan, bring reserved liquid back to a boil and add bouillon cubes, onion, and onion powder. Cook 5 to 10 minutes, or until onion is tender. Remove from heat and set aside. In large pot, mash potatoes and gradually add broth as necessary to obtain desired consistency. Serve.

*Serves 4*

# Sweet Potatoes with Apples

This sweet potato, apple, and cinnamon dish provides a refreshing change and goes well with beef and fish.

Cooking spray, for coating
⅛ cup Splenda
½ teaspoon ground nutmeg
½ teaspoon ground cinnamon
3 medium sweet potatoes, peeled and sliced lengthwise
    ¼" thick
2 medium apples, cored, peeled, and sliced ¼" thick
2 tablespoons butter

Preheat oven to 350 degrees.

Coat baking dish with cooking spray. In small bowl, mix Splenda, nutmeg, and cinnamon together. Cover bottom of dish with single layer of potatoes. Sprinkle with Splenda mixture. Add layer of apples. Dot with 1 tablespoon butter. Continue to layer potatoes, Splenda mixture, apples, and butter. Cover and bake 55 to 60 minutes, or until potatoes are tender. Serve.

*Serves 4*

# Au Gratin Cabbage

*K. Taptik, Sharpsville, Pennsylvania*

Cabbage is tasty and full of vital nutrients for a well-balanced diet. You might serve this dish with lean pork chops.

Cooking spray, for coating
⅓ cup shredded carrot
⅓ cup chopped green onion
2 cups chopped cabbage
1 egg, beaten
½ cup nonfat milk
1 teaspoon dried parsley
⅓ cup shredded Swiss cheese
2 tablespoons grated Parmesan cheese

Preheat oven to 350 degrees.

Coat skillet with cooking spray. Sauté carrot and onion over medium heat until tender. Add cabbage and cook until softened. In bowl, whisk egg, milk, parsley, Swiss cheese, and 1 tablespoon of Parmesan cheese. Place cabbage mixture in baking dish coated with cooking spray. Pour cheese-egg mixture over cabbage. Sprinkle remaining tablespoon of Parmesan over top. Bake, uncovered, 30 to 35 minutes. Serve.

*Serves 4 to 6*

# Bulgur Pilaf

This is a very versatile recipe. If you serve this dish with beef or pork, use beef broth instead of chicken broth.

Cooking spray, for coating
¼ medium onion, minced
½ red bell pepper, chopped
1 clove garlic, minced
1 cup uncooked cracked wheat bulgur
1 cup sliced mushrooms
2 cups 99 percent fat-free chicken broth
1 teaspoon salt
¼ teaspoon black pepper
½ teaspoon curry powder
⅛ teaspoon cayenne pepper
¼ cup raisins (optional)

Coat medium saucepan with cooking spray. Over medium heat, sauté onion, pepper, and garlic until tender but not browned, 4 or 5 minutes. Add bulgur and mushrooms and cook few minutes longer. Stir in broth, salt, pepper, curry powder, and cayenne. Over high heat, bring to a boil, then cover and reduce heat. Simmer 15 minutes. Remove from heat and stir in raisins, if desired. Cover again and let stand 5 minutes before serving.

Variations: You can substitute ¼ cup chopped green onion for the yellow onion. The red bell pepper can be replaced with chopped carrots and ¼ cup frozen peas. Omit raisins for this variation.

*Serves 4*

# Cheesy Baked Polenta

Polenta is a mild corn-based grain that is gaining popularity in the United States as a tasty side dish. The cheese and vegetables in this dish make it very flavorful. This is best alongside grilled chicken or beef.

3 cups nonfat milk

1 cup polenta

1 teaspoon salt

¾ cup grated cheddar cheese

1 cup corn

1 tablespoon (or to taste) chopped pickled jalapeño rings (optional)

1 cup drained and chopped roasted red pepper

2 tablespoons grated Parmesan cheese

Cooking spray, for coating

Preheat oven to 425 degrees.

In medium saucepan over medium heat, combine milk, polenta, and salt. Bring to a boil, stirring constantly, until mixture is very thick and pulls away from sides of pan, about 10 minutes. Remove from heat, stir in cheddar cheese, corn, jalapeño, red pepper, and Parmesan cheese.

Coat 8" x 8" or 9" x 9" baking dish with cooking spray. Pack polenta into dish and bake 25 minutes, or until golden brown. Serve.

*Serves 6*

# No Sugar Baked Beans

Baked beans are a big no-no on the No Flour, No Sugar Diet because they're full of sugar. However, this recipe uses fruit juice to sweeten the beans. Feel free to jazz it up with a dash of cayenne pepper.

Cooking spray, for coating
1 medium yellow onion, chopped
Two 15-ounce cans navy beans, drained and rinsed
1 teaspoon dry mustard
¼ cup diced lean ham
¾ to 1 cup unsweetened apple juice concentrate

Preheat oven to 350 degrees.

Coat medium saucepan with cooking spray. Cook onion over medium heat until tender but not browned, about 5 minutes. Remove from heat and stir in beans, mustard, and ham. Stir in apple juice, little at a time, until mixture is very moist but not runny. Transfer to 2-quart baking dish and cook 30 to 45 minutes, or until heated through. Serve.

*Serves 6*

**17**

# *Desserts*

We all love rich, luscious, calorie-laden desserts. They are almost an American tradition. Remember Mom saying, "Save room for dessert"? For those of us who wish to lose weight or simply to maintain a current weight we've struggled to reach, desserts can be a big challenge. We still want to indulge ourselves—but without the consequences of the enormous calorie count of most desserts. So what's the answer? Is it to deny yourself the pleasure of a satisfying dessert, night after dreary night? No, the answer is, as you've heard from me before, moderation. Follow along: I'll discuss reaching a happy medium.

## Alternatives to Flour and Sugar

I've included in this chapter some of my favorite no flour, no sugar dessert recipes. Here are a few quick ideas that you might want to try.

For some people, especially those raised or still living in European countries, dessert choices are often anything but overly sweet and full of empty calories. Consider the French, who may complete a meal with a small variety of cheeses and fruit wedges. If you wish to follow suit, you might start with a dinner plate in the middle of the table offering small portions of three or four different cheeses and cut-up fresh fruit. Supply each of your family members or guests with a dessert-size plate and small forks.

Consider including Brie, Gorgonzola, and Gruyère along with some of the good, low-fat cheeses now available. Mozzarella made from part skim milk and low-fat Swiss cheese are good choices. Combine soft, hard, mild, and robust. You can't go wrong. The fruit? How about apple or pear wedges? Pineapple or kiwifruit slices? Be sure the fruit is reasonably firm and not too ripe so it can be picked up without falling apart. What a pleasant diversion from more familiar possibilities.

Fruit salad makes a healthful dessert and it can be prepared in advance of the meal. Choose pineapple, red and green seedless grapes, kiwifruit, mango, or whatever is in season. Cut larger fruit into bite-size pieces. If you choose to include bananas, wait to slice them until just before serving to keep them from turning brown. Dress up this colorful completion to your meal by serving it in long-stemmed wine-glasses. This makes the dessert seem extra special. See my Fruit and Yogurt Salad for a variation on this theme.

A berry-yogurt treat made with unsweetened frozen berries blended with nonfat plain yogurt makes an attractive and flavorful dessert that can be tossed together quickly. Mix equal parts (or to taste) and puree in your blender until the mixture is the consistency of pudding. Of course if fresh berries are available, use them. Use nonfat vanilla yogurt if you prefer. Garnish with a sprig of peppermint or a whole berry. Don't say that you used nonfat yogurt and no one will ever know.

This dessert is colorful, low cal, and sugar free (except for the natural sugars in the fruit). Make enough to have leftovers for breakfast the next morning.

Another easy dessert using nonfat yogurt is made with sugar-free gelatin. Prepare a box of flavored gelatin according to the package directions and chill until it just begins to set. Then stir in eight ounces of yogurt, combining well. Pour into fancy dishes and chill until set. Lemon- or lime-flavored gelatin is great for this, or if you really want more flavor, use no-sugar-added peach-flavored gelatin with sugar-free, low-fat peach yogurt.

If you wish to get creative, make one flavor yogurt-gelatin mix, allow to set in the dish, then pour a second-flavored mix over the first and allow it to set. Add a third and a fourth layer if you like. This makes colorful layers that are nearly as fun to serve as to eat.

## Or Try Some of My Recipes

My Brandied Apple Oven Soufflé is great for parties. The combination of apples infused with cinnamon, brandy, and the zest of an orange will take a few minutes to prepare but is certainly worth the compliments your guests will shower upon you. Give this one a try when the boss comes over.

My Spiced Peaches can be made and refrigerated the night before. Visualize a peach half infused with red wine, a cinnamon stick, lemon zest, and orange juice concentrate set before you. It sounds good, smells good, looks good, and *is* good.

Whatever your dessert—simple Baked Apples or a more complex Mandarin Mousse—make sure your choice complements the meal that precedes it. If your main course was heavy, keep this course light. Present it attractively and you'll be pleased with your creation, as will your family or guests.

# Apple Crisp

*Barbara J. Harris, Havelock, North Carolina*

Everyone loves the smell of apple crisp cooking, and the delightful taste that follows. This recipe eliminates flour and utilizes the taste of oats.

5 cups sliced tart apples
¾ cup sugar-free syrup
1 teaspoon ground cinnamon
1 cup Quaker regular oats
½ cup Splenda
4 tablespoons butter
Pinch of salt
8 tablespoons sugar-free whipped topping

Preheat oven to 375 degrees.

Place sliced apples in 8" x 8" pan. Cover with syrup and cinnamon. Mix well.

Put oats in blender and blend until crumbled. Amount should reduce to ¾ cup. Transfer to small bowl and add Splenda, butter, and salt. Blend until crumbly. Spread evenly over apples. Bake 35 minutes.

Remove from oven and allow to cool. Serve with sugar-free whipped topping.

*Serves 6 to 8*

# Mixed Berry Pudding

Who doesn't like raspberry chocolate pudding—especially when it is filled with fresh berries? If it's not the season for fresh berries, it's fine to substitute a frozen mixture.

2 cups water
One 1.2-ounce package sugar-free, fat-free chocolate
    pudding
One 0.3-ounce package sugar-free raspberry gelatin
12 ounces fresh berries to include raspberries, blueberries,
    sliced strawberries, and blackberries
Spearmint leaves, for garnish

Place room temperature water in saucepan. Add dry pudding and gelatin mixes. Cook over medium heat until thick and at boiling temperature. Remove from heat and cool. Add berries, mixing well. Cover. Divide into 4 wineglasses. Cover with plastic wrap and place in refrigerator 2 hours or overnight. Garnish each with spearmint leaf for a touch of elegance before serving.

*Serves 4*

# Banana Oatmeal Cookies

These cookies are a healthful alternative to traditional oatmeal raisin cookies. I promise you will not miss the flour.

3 ripe bananas
2 cups quick-cooking oats
1 cup chopped walnuts
½ cup raisins
1 teaspoon ground cinnamon
1 teaspoon vanilla extract
¼ teaspoon salt

Preheat oven to 350 degrees.

Grease cookie sheet.

Mash bananas in large bowl. Add remaining ingredients. With tablespoon, drop batter onto greased cookie sheet, flattening each dollop slightly. Bake 10 to 15 minutes, or until centers are firm. Cookies taste best well done and crispy.

*Makes 36 cookies*

# Pumpkin Pie Ramekins

*Lois Friss, Thousand Oaks, California*

Think of the smell of pumpkin pie wafting through your kitchen. Your family and friends will love this delightful dish.

¾ cup Equal
2 teaspoons pumpkin pie spice
2 eggs
One 15-ounce can pumpkin
One 12-ounce can evaporated skim milk

Preheat oven to 425 degrees.

Blend Equal and pumpkin spice in small bowl.

In separate large bowl, beat eggs. Add Equal and pumpkin spice mixture to eggs. Mix in pumpkin. Gradually stir in evaporated milk.

Spoon into 8 ramekins. Place in pan with water halfway up sides of ramekins.

Bake 10 minutes. Reduce temperature to 350 degrees and bake 30 minutes longer. Cool and remove ramekins from pan. Serve either warm or cool.

*Serves 8*

# Mixed Fruit Medley

This delicious blend of spiced apples and peaches will prove to be a favorite. It's easy to prepare and can be assembled early and popped into the oven at your convenience. It's a real crowd-pleaser.

2 apples, cored, peeled, and cut into chunks
1 cup red raspberries

1 cup blueberries
One 7-ounce can peaches, unsweetened, with juice
¼ teaspoon ground cinnamon
¼ teaspoon ground nutmeg

Preheat oven to 350 degrees.

Place all ingredients in 8" x 8" baking dish. Sprinkle spices over top. Bake 15 to 20 minutes. Serve.

*Serves 4*

# Peanut Butter Cookies

If your family loves peanut butter cookies, this recipe can easily be doubled or tripled. Store any leftovers in a sealed container to retain freshness.

1 cup sugar-free peanut butter
1 egg
1 cup Splenda
Cooking spray, for coating

Preheat oven to 375 degrees.

Combine all ingredients and roll dough into 2" balls. Place on cookie sheet coated with cooking spray. Flatten slightly with tines of fork. Bake 10 minutes. Cool and remove with spatula to prevent breaking. Serve.

*Makes 8 to 10 cookies*

# Baked Apples

This dessert is reminiscent of fall, but it can be prepared at any time of the year.

4 tablespoons butter
4 tablespoons Splenda
½ teaspoon ground cinnamon
½ teaspoon ground nutmeg
½ teaspoon ground allspice
4 large apples, washed and cored
Cooking spray, for coating

Preheat oven to 350 degrees.

Blend butter, Splenda, and spices in small bowl. Divide evenly into apples. Place filled apples in baking dish coated with cooking spray and bake 30 minutes, or until apples are tender. Serve warm.

*Serves 4*

# Peach Pudding

Peaches remind us of summertime. This dish can be served year-round to bring summer memories to a cold winter day.

2 cups water
One 1.2-ounce package sugar-free vanilla pudding
One 0.3-ounce package sugar-free peach gelatin
1½ cups chopped fresh or sugar-free canned peaches
Ground cinnamon, for garnish

Place water in small pan. Add pudding and gelatin. Cook over medium heat until mixture reaches a boil. Remove and cool. Stir in peaches. Cover and refrigerate until ready to serve. Serve in individual dessert dishes, garnished with dashes of cinnamon.

*Serves 4 to 6*

# Crème Brûlée

*Barb Carter, Port Saint Lucie, Florida*

This exquisite dessert delights everyone finding it on a restaurant menu at the end of a meal. Just imagine the pleasure your dinner guests will experience knowing you took the extra time and effort to prepare this.

3 eggs, at room temperature
1 teaspoon vanilla extract
$^1/_3$ cup Splenda
2½ cups regular or soy milk, scalded
Ground nutmeg

Preheat oven to 350 degrees.

Beat eggs. Add vanilla and Splenda. Slowly add scalded milk until blended. Pour mixture into individual custard cups. Sprinkle nutmeg over tops. Place cups in baking dish. Fill dish with water to within ½" of top of cups. Bake 45 minutes. Cool. Refrigerate until ready to serve cold.

*Serves 4*

# Brandied Apple Oven Soufflé

Don't let the idea of separating eggs scare you. Just be sure not to break the yolks. This is a beautiful dessert for parties or a great brunch course. Carefully follow the directions to avoid a collapsed soufflé, which still tastes delicious but is not as attractive.

Cooking spray, for coating
2 small apples, cored, peeled, and thinly sliced
2 tablespoons brandy
1 teaspoon orange zest
1 tablespoon sugar-free apple juice concentrate
Dash of ground cinnamon
½ cup plus 1 to 2 tablespoons water
4 eggs, separated
1 individual packet Splenda
¼ teaspoon vanilla extract
Dash of salt

Preheat oven to 350 degrees.

Coat skillet with cooking spray. In small pot, simmer apples, brandy, orange zest, apple juice, and cinnamon over medium-high heat, about 5 minutes. If liquid evaporates before apples are tender, add 1 tablespoon water at a time to keep moist. Remove from heat and cover. Set aside.

Beat egg yolks, Splenda, and vanilla in small bowl, using electric mixer, 1 to 2 minutes.

In large mixing bowl, with clean beaters, whip egg whites with ½ cup water and salt until stiff peaks form. Carefully fold few spoonfuls of whites into yolk mixture. Then very carefully fold remaining yolk mixture into whites. (This is known as tempering which allows 2 mixtures to be successfully combined without "deflating" or "breaking" either.)

Coat clean oven-safe skillet with cooking spray. Pour in fluffy egg mixture. Smooth out top with a spatula. Cook about 3 minutes on stovetop over medium-high heat until underside is browned. Place skillet in top portion of oven and bake 10 to 12 minutes until done. Soufflé is done when knife inserted into center of dish comes out clean. Remove from oven.

Slide soufflé onto serving dish and spread apple mixture on top. Serve at once.

*Serves 4*

# Fruity Rice Pudding

This dish also works well as a breakfast course. Vary the dried fruits according to your tastes, but blueberries and apricots always blend well together.

2 cups evaporated skim milk
$1/3$ cup unsweetened apple juice
1 egg, beaten
1 teaspoon vanilla extract
3 cups cooked rice
½ cup dried blueberries
½ cup chopped dried apricots
Cooking spray, for coating
¼ teaspoon ground cinnamon

Preheat oven to 325 degrees.

Mix milk, apple juice, egg, and vanilla in large bowl until well blended. Stir in rice and fruit. Coat 2-quart baking dish with cooking spray. Pour in rice mixture.

Bake 20 minutes, stirring once. Sprinkle with cinnamon.

Bake 35 to 40 minutes longer until milk is absorbed. Remove from oven. Serve warm or chilled.

*Serves 8*

# Frozen Banana Pops

This recipe can be modified to be kid friendly if you drizzle the frozen bananas with dark chocolate sauce.

4 large ripe bananas
8 Popsicle sticks
2 cups nonfat plain yogurt
1 cup unsweetened shredded coconut

Peel bananas and cut in half crosswise. Put 1 stick into each half, entering from the cut end.

Pour yogurt into shallow bowl and place coconut in another shallow bowl. Coat bananas with yogurt, then dredge through coconut. Lay bananas on baking sheet covered with waxed paper. Freeze 1 hour. Wrap tightly with foil or freezer wrap. Return to freezer until ready to eat.

*Serves 8*

# Spiced Peaches

This dessert is good for dinner parties since it can be prepared in advance. If you like, place a dollop of sugar-free whipped topping on each serving.

½ cup hearty red wine
1 whole cinnamon stick
1 teaspoon lemon juice
1 teaspoon lemon zest
2 tablespoons unsweetened orange juice concentrate
4 peaches, halved, pitted, and peeled

Mix wine, cinnamon, lemon juice and zest, and orange juice in small saucepan. Bring mixture to a boil. Then reduce heat and simmer 3 to 5 minutes until syrupy in consistency. Place each peach half in bowl. Pour wine sauce over and let sit at room temperature at least 2 hours. You can refrigerate this dish, covered, overnight, but bring to room temperature before serving.

*Serves 8*

# Blueberry Raspberry Crumble

This colorful dish is simple to prepare and nutritious as well. It's a great idea for a summer picnic dish.

Cooking spray, for coating
½ pint fresh or frozen blueberries (about 1 cup)
½ pint fresh or frozen raspberries (about 1 cup)
¼ cup plus 2 tablespoons Splenda
2 tablespoons cornstarch
¼ cup chopped walnuts
½ cup uncooked old-fashioned oatmeal
2 tablespoons butter, melted

Preheat oven to 350 degrees.

Coat baking dish with cooking spray.

Combine blueberries, raspberries, ¼ cup Splenda, and cornstarch in bowl. Pour into baking dish.

In separate small bowl, mix walnuts, oatmeal, remaining Splenda, and butter. Sprinkle over berry mixture and bake 30 minutes. Serve warm.

*Serves 3 to 4*

# Strawberry Gelatin with Applesauce

The blending of gelatin and applesauce creates a unique texture.

2 cups water
One 0.3-ounce package sugar-free strawberry gelatin
1 cup sugar-free applesauce
1 pound fresh strawberries, sliced, with 2 whole berries
    reserved
Spearmint or peppermint leaves, for garnish

Boil water and dissolve gelatin according to package directions. Add applesauce and sliced berries. Pour into shallow serving dish and refrigerate until ready to serve.

To serve, slice 2 reserved berries into quarters from bottom up, not severing top. Fan with fingers to make flower petals and place on top of dish. Add spearmint or peppermint leaves for leaf effect.

*Serves 4 to 6*

# Banana Bread

Who would ever think banana bread would be included in a no flour, no sugar cookbook? Well, oatmeal offers a nice substitute for flour.

2 eggs
4 ripe bananas
1 cup uncooked old-fashioned oatmeal
½ cup wheat germ
⅓ cup extra virgin olive oil
½ cup Splenda
1 teaspoon baking powder
½ teaspoon baking soda
½ teaspoon salt
1 teaspoon ground cinnamon
1 teaspoon ground nutmeg
½ cup chopped walnuts
Cooking spray, for coating

Preheat oven to 375 degrees.

In large bowl, beat eggs. In small bowl, mash bananas and add to eggs. Add remaining ingredients except cooking spray to bowl, blending well. Pour into 4" x 8" loaf pan coated with cooking spray. Bake 40 to 45 minutes. Serve either warm or cool.

*Serves 8*

# Fruit and Yogurt Salad

This is a simple dish to prepare, yet the results are very rewarding.

3 apples, cored, peeled, and cut into bite-size pieces
½ pound unsweetened pineapple chunks, drained
¼ pound red seedless grapes
½ cup chopped walnuts
1½ cups sugar-free vanilla yogurt
2 teaspoons bran buds, for garnish

Combine all ingredients except bran buds in bowl. Refrigerate until ready to serve. Add ½ teaspoon bran buds to each serving as garnish.

*Serves 4 to 6*

# Zippy Orange Rice Custard

Mild brown rice really picks up on the flavors and spices in this dish.

3 eggs, at room temperature
1½ teaspoons vanilla extract
2 cups nonfat milk
¼ cup Splenda
2 tablespoons orange zest
2 tablespoons unsweetened orange juice concentrate
1 cup cooked brown rice
1 teaspoon ground cinnamon
1 teaspoon ground nutmeg

Preheat oven to 350 degrees.

Beat eggs in 2-quart baking dish. Add vanilla, milk, Splenda, orange zest and juice, and rice. Mix well. Bake 20 minutes. Stir dish, bringing rice up from bottom to blend with other ingredients. Sprinkle cinnamon and nutmeg over top, return to oven, and bake another 20 minutes. Serve warm or cold.

*Serves 3 to 4*

# Flourless Oatmeal Bars

This dish is a great one to have on hand to enjoy with tea after dinner. It's easy to prepare and will store well for several days in your refrigerator.

Cooking spray, for coating
1 teaspoon vanilla extract
$1/3$ cup extra virgin olive oil
½ cup unsweetened applesauce
1 egg, at room temperature
$1/3$ cup Splenda
½ teaspoon salt
1 teaspoon ground cinnamon
2 cups uncooked quick-cooking oatmeal
1½ teaspoons baking soda
¾ cup nonfat milk

Preheat oven to 350 degrees.

Coat 9" x 9" baking dish with cooking spray.

In large bowl, blend vanilla, oil, applesauce, egg, Splenda, salt, and cinnamon. Stir in oatmeal, baking soda, and milk, mixing well. Pour into dish and bake 25 to 30 minutes. Cool and cut into bars. Store leftovers, if there are any, in a covered container.

*Makes 12 bars*

# Drunken Strawberries

This adult-only dessert is sweet, crunchy, and definitely party friendly.

2 tablespoons pine nuts
2 cups sliced fresh strawberries
2 kiwifruit, peeled and sliced
¼ cup dark rum

Toast pine nuts in dry skillet over medium heat until beginning to turn golden. Remove from skillet immediately. Set aside.

Blend strawberries, kiwifruit, and rum in serving bowl. Cover and chill 1 hour but not more than 3. Before serving, sprinkle nuts on top.

*Serves 8*

# Blender Banana Shakes

Bananas have more potassium than orange juice has, and this recipe has both. You'll feel good when you have this for dessert.

4 ripe bananas
½ cup unsweetened orange juice concentrate
2 cups evaporated skim milk
2 cups nonfat plain yogurt
8 fresh raspberries or strawberries, for garnish

Combine bananas, orange juice, milk, and yogurt in blender or food processor. Blend until smooth. Pour into 4 tall glasses and garnish each with 2 berries.

*Serves 4*

# Mandarin Mousse

Use fresh mandarin oranges for the juice in this recipe. Or if you can find canned mandarin oranges without added sugar, drain them and use as a substitute.

1 teaspoon orange zest
1¼ cups orange juice
12 individual packets Splenda
Dash of salt
1 tablespoon arrowroot powder
1 egg, beaten
1 tablespoon lime juice
1 teaspoon unflavored gelatin
¼ cup cold water
¼ cup evaporated skim milk
¼ cup nonfat sour cream
½ cup fresh raspberries, for garnish

In medium saucepan, mix orange zest, 1 cup orange juice, 11 packets Splenda, salt, and arrowroot. Bring to a boil over medium heat and stir until mixture thickens. Remove from heat.

In small bowl, stir large spoonful of hot mixture into the beaten egg. Add egg mixture to the saucepan, stirring constantly. Return to heat and cook until mixture comes to a boil, stirring constantly. Remove from heat and add lime juice and remaining orange juice. Let cool to room temperature.

Sprinkle gelatin over cold water in small bowl. Let stand 4 minutes until softened. Set bowl over small pan of simmering water and stir until gelatin dissolves, 2 to 3 minutes. Cool.

In large bowl, beat milk and sour cream with electric mixer until creamy. Add remaining Splenda and beat until soft peaks form. Beat in gelatin mixture. Fold creamy mixture into orange mixture.

Spoon into 4 serving bowls and chill 2 hours, or until set. Serve garnished with raspberries.

*Serves 4*

# Fruity Frappe

This recipe is good for a summer afternoon snack or dessert. It's always nice when you can get a sweet treat that's full of fruity goodness.

15 ice cubes
1 cup evaporated skim milk
1 tablespoon vanilla extract
1 medium banana
1 cup still-frozen unsweetened mixed berries

In blender or food processor, crush ice. Add other ingredients and blend until fairly smooth. Pour into 2 tall glasses and serve.

*Serves 2*

# Cheese Board

This is a traditional European dessert and many find it more satisfying than a sweet dessert. Try to vary the types of cheese you serve, including a soft cheese (Brie), a strongly flavored cheese (Gorgonzola), and a milder cheese (Gruyère). The fruit should be firm.

2 ounces Brie cheese, sliced

2 ounces Gorgonzola cheese, sliced

2 ounces Gruyère cheese, sliced

2 medium apples, cored, sliced, and tossed with 1 tablespoon
   lemon juice

2 pears, cored, peeled, and sliced

Arrange cheeses on serving platter in attractive pattern with fruit.

*Serves 4*

# INDEX